# Welfare Economics and Externalities In An Open Ended Universe: A Modern Austrian Perspective

# Welfare Economics and Externalities In An Open Ended Universe: A Modern Austrian Perspective

**Roy E. Cordato, Ph.D.**

Foreword by
Professor Dominick T. Armentano
University of Hartford

Springer Science+Business Media, LLC

**Library of Congress Cataloging-in-Publication Data**

Cordato, Roy E.
Welfare economics and externalities in an open ended universe : a modern Austrian perspective / Roy E. Cordato : foreword by Dominick T. Armentano.
p. cm.
Includes bibliographical references and index.
ISBN 978-1-4757-2147-8 ISBN 978-1-4757-2145-4 (eBook)
DOI 10.1007/978-1-4757-2145-4
1. Welfare economics. 2. Externalities (Economics) 3. Austrian school of economists. I. Title.
HB846.C67 1992
330.15'7--dc20 92-19778
CIP

---


Originally published by Kluwer Academic Publishers in 1992
Softcover reprint of the hardcover 1st edition 1992



*Printed on acid-free paper.*

To Karen and Stephanie

# CONTENTS

# FOREWORD: PROPERTY RIGHTS, EFFICIENCY, AND SOCIAL WELFARE

by Dominick T. Armentano
University of Hartford

Since Adam Smith, economists have been sympathetic to the idea that the selfish pursuit of profit by individuals can enhance the overall economic welfare of society. The easiest way to understand this notion is to assume that when individuals trade and exchange, they tend to give up resources or goods that they value less for resources or goods that they value more. Thus the process of exchange itself may be able to enhance the net welfare of each participating individual and, generalizing to all exchanges, the welfare of society as a whole.

**Externalities and Public Policy**

There is still much disagreement and debate concerning this general proposition. One of the most important areas of contention concerns the issue of market externalities. Briefly put, not all of the costs and benefits of individual trades are necessarily internalized by the traders. Some benefits and costs may leak off and affect the behavior of other individuals who are not a direct party to the exchange. Political economy has long been concerned about these so-called "neighborhood effects" or "spillovers." For example, how should the liability for harmful spillovers be determined? How are private production and consumption decisions altered by positive and negative neighborhood effects? And if specific externalities are determined to be socially inefficient, what is the most appropriate public policy to restore market efficiency?

With regard to these issues, Roy Cordato's new book is both timely and important. Questions of liability and efficiency with respect to negative spillovers are current, cutting-edge public policy issues. In the area of industrial pollution especially, significant private and taxpayer resources have been committed to schemes to redress the "social costs" of alleged environmental degradation. In addition, government agencies and the courts are increasingly regulating private behavior in this area. Thus it is important to reexamine the economic rationale for regulating externalities and whether existing public policy is appropriate.

## Market Failure and Catallactic Efficiency

Aside from the specific issue of externalities, this volume is also important because it attempts to provide an alternative paradigm to the conventional neoclassical welfare analysis. Most economists still "do" efficiency and welfare analysis by comparing existing market conduct and performance to conditions that would exist under perfect competition with perfect information. Markets are said to be efficient if market price and marginal cost are equal; if this equality does not hold, however, then markets are said to "fail" (market failure) and this can rationalize remedial public policy.

Now to be sure, the perfectly competitive benchmark has come in for some extensive criticism over the years, especially from Austrian economists. Yet the paradigm has (somehow) managed to survive all of the criticism. One reason for that survival may be that it has been unclear to economists (even Austrian economists) what alternative approach, if any, could replace the standard Pigouvian methodology.

The truly innovative part of Cordato's book is a spirited attack on the conventional welfare paradigm (including the Coase theorem) and a serious attempt to recast conventional efficiency and welfare economics along Austrian lines. The foundations of the Austrian methodology are individualism and subjectivism. For Austrians, human action must always be understood in terms of individual purposes, actions and goals. And, importantly, the gains or losses associated with individual action must always be considered personal, non-comparable, and non-additive.

These tenets are clear but they have always created a certain ambiguity in discussions of social efficiency or social welfare. Clearly, Austrians reject the conventional efficiency and welfare benchmark since it assumes perfect information, abstracts from time, and makes the end-state equilibrium condition inevitable. Contrariwise, Austrians tend to see competition as a discovery (of information) process that unfolds through time and is inevitably open-ended. In addition, Austrians reject the social cost/benefit methodology since it is based explicitly on illegitimate inter-personal value comparisons and upon aggregation. Yet having acknowledged that the conventional welfare analysis is inherently faulty, it has never been precisely clear what an economist from a subjectivist perspective could say concerning overall efficiency and welfare.

He might, of course, assume that voluntary trade simply increases everyone's welfare ex ante; but this logic says nothing about the even more interesting ex post situations. Or he might assume that increasing information leads, necessarily, to an increase in the overall "coordination of individual plans" and, thus, to an increase in overall social welfare. But as Cordato argues, it is not obvious that increasing information always increases overall plan coordination; indeed, as the market process "grinds away," some previously coordinated plans will inevitably become discoordinated. Is there any appropriate perspective, then, for evaluating the efficiency and welfare of the entire market process?

Cordato attempts to solve the riddle by arguing that the efficiency of the entire social order must focus on the institutional property rights framework rather than on any particular market outcome. Since the market process is inherently open ended and never ending, focusing on an end-state equilibrium condition is irrelevant. And since the acquisition of knowledge is the micro-level efficiency problem, assuming perfect information (as conventional analysis does) must be misleading. Instead, social efficiency--or what Cordato terms "catallactic" efficiency--should focus on the extent to which the overall institutional framework promotes or retards the pursuit of individual plans at the micro-level by the traders involved. And this, in turn, will depend greatly upon whether the legal system is able to clearly define and strictly enforce individual rights to property.

**Competition, Monopoly, and Regulation**

This alternative approach to social efficiency and welfare analysis has broad applications well beyond the issue of externalities. Its most obvious area of application is to questions of competition, monopoly, and antitrust policy. Industrial organization and public policy have long been dominated by Pigouvian welfare analysis and discussions of "market failure." The structure, conduct and performance of real world firms are always being compared to structure, conduct and performance under conditions of perfect competition. Markets are said to "fail" when price and marginal cost are not equal; or when products are not homogeneous; or when firms make "extraordinary" profits in the "long run;" or when market output is "restricted" from output under perfectly competitive conditions.

The majority of industrial organization economists implicitly assume that individual costs and benefits are objective, comparable, and capable of aggregation. Monopoly is always said to reduce consumer welfare--as if the utility of individual consumers could be totaled into some meaningful aggregate and compared at different points in time. Monopoly is said to enhance the welfare of the producers--as if the utility of the producers could be totaled both before and after some price increase. And finally overall social welfare is said to be reduced by monopoly power--the so-called "dead weight" welfare loss triangle--again as if we could add together the individual (e)valuations associated with any "lost output."

Policy analysis in antitrust and in other regulatory areas has been derived explicitly from the efficiency analysis outlined above. The legal restriction of business mergers, price discrimination, tying agreements, and especially price-fixing (collusion) all relate directly to efficiency conditions under perfect competition and to Pigouvian cost/benefit analysis. It is interesting to note that the so-called "antitrust revolution" that modestly slowed federal antitrust enforcement in the 1980's did not seriously challenge the foundations of the conventional efficiency and welfare analysis itself. Indeed, the currently popular "rule of reason" analysis in antitrust is based explicitly on the Pigouvian paradigm.

Seen from Cordato's perspective, the bulk of industrial organization analysis and the consequent policy pronouncements are totally without scientific foundation. Catallactic efficiency would require that the legal framework encourage individuals to pursue their own goals as consistently as possible. Catallactic efficiency would require that the legal framework facilitate the discovery and use of physical and intellectual property. Thus it would be socially inefficient to have the legal system interfere with individual plan coordination--as antitrust policy generally does--or interfere with the discovery, dissemination, and use of information.

As an example, take the per se prohibition against horizontal price collusion, the most widely supported antitrust restriction. The traditional Pigouvian rationale for the prohibition is that such agreements, if effective, will reduce consumer and social welfare. Even those few analysts who dissent from this position tend to argue entirely within the Piguovian paradigm. They hold either that collusion will lower "costs" or that price and output agreements between competitors will be unstable and quickly "break down." Despite their differences, therefore, both sides are in conceptual agreement that a "naked" price and output agreement that does not achieve lower costs or does not "break down" must be inefficient and socially undesirable.

From a catallactic perspective the issue of social efficiency would be seen very differently. In the first place it would be impossible to compare the aggregate welfare of consumers (and producers) before and after any increase in price and, thus, impossible to conclude that business collusion reduces social welfare. Second, and more fundamentally, the act of (price) agreement is explicit evidence of social cooperation and plan coordination. A price agreement, like any contract, is simply a "means" that aims to enhance the individual welfare "ends" of the parties involved. In direct contrast to the Pigouvian position, therefore, a price and output agreement that actually accomplishes its objectives is precisely efficient while an agreement that is unstable or "breaks down" is not efficient. Finally, any government policy that either mandates or prohibits any collusive agreement would, itself, contribute directly to market inefficiency.

A thorough-going catallactic perspective would completely transform industrial organization theory and regulatory policy. For instance, all business mergers and all joint ventures would be seen as socially efficient arrangements aimed at achieving some mutually determined business goal; they no longer could be restricted by law in the name of efficiency. In addition, the long-standing industrial organization anxiety over highly differentiated products would be seen as a thoroughly illegitimate quibbling over ends, not means. Finally, the traditional antitrust concern with market share, concentration, and "entry barriers" would be seen as entirely misplaced. Any market share and any degree of market concentration would simply be the necessary outcome of an open market process of voluntary plan coordination. And the only efficiency-relevant entry barriers would be those associated with legal restrictions that prevent opportunities for additional seller/consumer coordination.

The catallactic theory of efficiency would also (finally) allow an unambiguous definition of the concepts "competition" and "monopoly." Competition--encompassing both rivalry and cooperation--would be seen as an open-ended process of (information) discovery and (plan) adjustment without any legal prohibition. Monopoly (power), in turn, would then be defined as a situation where legal barriers prevent business organizations from discovering and utilizing information or attempting to coordinate their resource and product plans with those of other firms or consumers. Thus (legal) monopoly would still be socially undesirable because it would (still) lower economic efficiency and social welfare.

Does the catallactic perspective leave any role for government regulation in the antitrust area? Not much. The only application of antitrust policy to promote efficiency might involve the use of antitrust against any federal, state, or local legal restrictions that inhibit opportunities for individual plan making among market participants. (Ending state or local cable t.v. legal monopoly would be an example.) These legal restrictions, in the conventional lexicon, are all "restraints of trade" and they all promote market inefficiency. If the bulk of private and public antitrust regulation, itself so destructive of social efficiency, cannot be immediately repealed--as it should be--then at least it might be employed to remove other legal barriers to trade and exchange.

**Conclusion**

In conclusion, the efficiency and welfare methodology that Cordato proposes can be usefully applied to an examination of policy issues well beyond the question of market externalities. Indeed, it is to be hoped that this book will inspire additional research programs that critically examine other alleged "market failures" while they expand and deepen our understanding of the relationship between property rights and social efficiency.

---

Dominick T. Armentano is a professor of economics at the University of Hartford, West Hartford, Connecticut. He is the author of *Antitrust and Monopoly: Anatomy of a Policy Failure*, Second Edition, (New York and London: Holmes and Meier, 1990) and *Antitrust Policy: The Case for Repeal*, (Washington: Cato Institute, 1991).

# PREFACE

In 1978 I was taking a microeconomics course in my masters program at the University of Hartford and we were covering the issues of perfect competition and economic efficiency. At this same time I had begun to familiarize myself with some of the Austrian school economists particularly Hayek, Kirzner, and Rothbard and I was having many very enlightening conversations with Professor Armentano, who was also on the U of H faculty. In the micro class discussions I began to raise all of the arguments against the perfect competition model that I had been reading about in the Austrian literature. The professor in the class, a very patient and tolerant man (in addition to being a fine economist), Professor Bharat Kolluri, listened to my arguments against the standard view of efficiency and then asked, "but what do you have to offer in its place?" I hemmed and hawed and babbled something, but I realized that I had no answer. In a real sense it was Professor Kolluri's question that ultimately led to this book.

The following semester I took an excellent course in public finance with Professor John Sullivan where this situation repeated itself. This time it was with respect to discussions of externalities and public goods. I realized that, given my developing Austrian perspective, the standard arguments regarding these issues broke every rule in the book, especially those regarding the subjective nature of costs and benefits. On the other hand all my responses were in the form of criticism, I had no alternative to offer.

At this point I decided that I needed to find out what Austrians had to offer with regards to a positive theory of efficiency. After all, efficiency opens the door for an economist, qua economist, to talk about public policy. Oddly enough I found the word was almost completely absent from the Austrian literature. It does not appear in the index of any of the major Austrian writings, including Mises' *Human Action* or Rothbard's *Man, Economy, and State*.[1] While in both of these works, and in much of the Austrian literature, there seemed to be some concept of efficiency that was being implied, there was no explicit discussion of the issue, other than in critical terms. Indeed, while Austrians had correctly identified a host of fundamental flaws in the standard analysis based on perfect competition, there was no approach that was being offered as a viable alternative.

At that time the only place in the Austrian literature that I could find an alternative theory of efficiency specifically discussed was in a little known and out of print book by Israel Kirzner, *Market Theory and the Price System* (1963).

Here, invoking a strictly Misesian perspective, Kirzner carefully laid out definitions for both individual and social efficiency. I was amazed that this was the only place in the Austrian economics literature that the notion of efficiency was specifically defined (in a way that completely rejected perfect competition I might add) and no one (Austrian or not) seemed to have noticed. Certainly the theory had not been applied to the traditional areas where efficiency is a concern for economists in general. How do we define competition and monopoly? How would externalities, free rider problems, and public goods be viewed in light of Kirzner's "Austrian" theory of efficiency? These questions inspired me to write a paper for a seminar class in public finance, under the direction of Professor Sullivan, titled "The Austrian Theory of Efficiency and the Role of Government," which went on to be published in the *Journal of Libertarian Studies* (1980) and was my first published article. In retrospect, it is clear that this paper was an attempt to respond to Professor Kolluri's original question.

In my naivete I thought that this article would bring to light Kirzner's neglected theory and that suddenly Austrians would start invoking the theory everywhere when talking about public policy. As it turned out, the only person who seemed to notice was Professor Armentano who explicitly invoked the theory, citing both my paper and Kirzner's original 1963 discussion, in his book, *Antitrust and Monopoly*, which appeared in 1982 (2nd ed., 1990).

At about this same time, a collection of articles was published, edited by Mario Rizzo (1979) in which the subject of efficiency was the topic of hot debate. This debate took place between Harold Demsetz, who was attempting to make a case for a Coasean-type cost-benefit approach to efficiency, and Austrian economists John Egger, Murray Rothbard, and Mario Rizzo who were making the arguments against such an approach. The conclusion reached by the three Austrians, which seemed to take hold among Austrian economists in general, was that the concept of efficiency should be thrown out all together--that public policy was primarily a question for ethics, not economics.[2] This view has always struck me as inappropriate, for a very pragmatic reason: if Austrian economists were ever going to be able to enter debates concerning public policy, and be listened to by other economists, we would have to be able to talk about efficiency. And if we couldn't accept the standard view of efficiency then we would have to offer an alternative.

As I went on to work on my Ph.D. at George Mason University I continued my interest in efficiency theory and was anxious to take every opportunity to talk about the concept with my professors. At GMU it was Professor Jack High who was most interested in the issue. At the time he was concerned about Kirzner's concept of coordination which forms the foundation for Kirzner's theory of social efficiency. It was Professor High who first inspired me to think critically about Professor Kirzner's approach to efficiency. Many of the issues that I raise in chapter 2 of this book concerning Kirzner's coordination standard have their roots in these discussions with Jack High. They were also significantly influenced by a paper that Jack had just written for a volume in honor of Ludwig Lachmann, titled "Equilibrium and Disequilibrium in the Market Process" (1986). But while Jack was taking the Rothbardian position that efficiency should be jettisoned from policy analysis, I was still convinced that it was an important concept for Austrians to develop.

From the perspective of this book the penultimate project for me was my dissertation, *An Analysis of Externalities in Austrian Economics* (1987). Primarily an exercise in the history of economic thought on the issue, this allowed me to sort through the entire issue of efficiency and externalities analysis from an Austrian perspective. The dissertation forced me to identify exactly what Austrians were saying on these issues and more importantly it allowed me to pinpoint the gaps in the analysis. I realized that while Austrians had offered alternative visions of efficiency and welfare economics (Kirzner and Rothbard respectively) and an alternative assessment of externalities, (in Mises and Rothbard) there was no attempt to connect the two. Also, that project made me realize that the concept of efficiency, which must form the foundation of any normative economic analysis of externalities, needed to be reconsidered and overhauled.

All of this has led to this book, especially the theory of catallactic efficiency presented in chapter 3. My hope is that Austrian economists in general reconsider the value of having a strong theory of efficiency as part of their analytical tool kit. I not only hope that, ultimately, we can persuade the economics profession that the perfectly competitive general equilibrium presents a fundamentally flawed perspective on efficiency, but that the disequilibrium world view of Austrian economics offers a more fruitful and relevant context for judging social welfare.

## NOTES

1 While Rothbard had presented a positive theory of welfare economics [1977 (1956)] in terms of "social utility" he did not invoke the concept of efficiency while doing so. In fact, in a later paper he explicitly rejects the concept as a welfare guide (1973B).

2 This view has its roots in Rothbard, 1973B.

## ACKNOWLEDGEMENTS

There are a great number of people whose efforts and sacrifices have gone into helping me complete this project. First I would like to thank my wife Karen Palasek and my daughter Stephanie for their indulgence while this book has been in process. They were willing to sacrifice many weekends and holidays so that this project could be completed. Also I would like to thank my mother, Mary Cordato for her continuing support.

Thanks also should go to the folks at Kluwer Academic Publishers. In particular I would like to thank my editor Dave McConnell who believed strongly in this project from the day it was proposed to him and three anonymous referees whose positive reviews reaffirmed Dave's initial reaction.

Chapter 1 and to a great extent, chapter 2 were originally written as part of my dissertation. As such the writing of these chapters benefited greatly from the comments of my dissertation committee at George Mason University, namely Professors Donald Lavoie, Committee Chairman, and members Jack High and Chris Jones, at GMU, Professor Tom DiLorenzo, now at The University of Tennessee at Chattanooga, and Dwight Lee at the University of Georgia. As noted, this book is the culmination of research and thinking about the issues of efficiency, welfare economics, and externalities that began while I was working on my M.A. at the University of Hartford. In light of this I would like to thank Professors Bharat Kolluri and John Sullivan whose courses in microeconomics and public finance respectively inspired me to think seriously about these issues. My greatest debt of thanks goes to Professor Dominick Armentano. Intellectually he has always been my strongest supporter. Dom first introduced me to both economics in general and Austrian economics, and even when I was a lowly graduate student he was always willing to take my ideas seriously. In addition I would like to thank him for taking the time to write the "Foreword" to this book, it means a great deal to me.

Over the years I have benefited immensely from conversations with a number of economists and other scholars. Someone whose input has been very helpful, particularly with respect to the ideas in chapter 5 is Professor Michael Krauss from George Mason University School of Law. In addition to offering me valuable, thought provoking, and often unsettling comments on earlier drafts, he graciously allowed me to audit his course in tort law which gave me a much better understanding of some of the legal issue that I had to deal with. Of course, any short-comings in my understanding of these issues are completely my own responsibility. Professor Krauss and I still have some fundamental disagreements about the appropriate nature of property rights, but I am sure that is why I find our conversations about the subject so enjoyable. I would also like to thank my good friend Professor Peter Boettke at New York University for taking the time to read and offer comments on several chapters. In addition, I have benefited greatly from the many informal conversations that Pete and I have had over the years.

Thanks should also go to a number of other people who have influenced my thinking in ways that have had a positive effect on this project. In particular I would like to thank Professors Robert Ekelund and Roger Garrison at Auburn University, Professor William Butos at Trinity College, Professor Richard Langlois at The University of Connecticut, Dr. Norman Ture and Dr. Michael Schuyler at The Institute for Research on the Economics of Taxation, and Professor John Egger at Towson State University. I would also like to thank Professor Larry White at the University of Georgia who gave me valuable comments on chapter 1 when it was originally being prepared for my dissertation.

A special thanks should go to members of the Saturday Morning Austrian Colloquium in Fairfax, Va., particularly Joe Cobb, William Laffer, Ralph Rector, and Jeff Tucker, who have consistently been there to offer me very valuable comments on nearly all chapters in this book. I would also like to thank members of the Austrian Economics Colloquium at New York University, and the participants in student-faculty seminars at Auburn University and Trinity College in Hartford, Ct.

I would like to express my appreciation to my good friend Sheldon Richman. He has helped a great deal with the editing of this book, offering me comments and suggestions on every chapter. He has also given me valuable comments with respect to the content of the book, particularly in chapter 2.

Several organizations have given me moral and financial support that helped make this project a reality. First I would like to thank Llewllyn Rockwell and the Ludwig von Mises Institute. The Mises Institute demonstrated its confidence in this project well before any contracts were signed. For this I am grateful. I would also like to thank Walter Grinder and the Institute for Humane Studies for both specific support on this project and for financial support that the Institute has provided me over the years, and Laissez Faire Books for the commitment that it has made to this project. Finally I would like to thank The Center for the Study of Market Processes at George Mason University for the financial support and intellectual environment that it provided for me as a graduate student, which, directly and indirectly has had a positive impact on this project.

There are a group of people who have helped me keep my sanity during the course of this project. Special thanks goes out to Chuck Shorter, Will Dunham, Howard Stern, and Ric Flair. These folks all made it possible for me to "lighten-up."

Finally, I must thank those Austrian School economists, past and present, whose writings have laid the foundation for this project and whose shoulders I stand on; especially, Ludwig von Mises, Frederick Hayek, Israel Kirzner, Murray Rothbard, Ludwig Lachmann, Mario Rizzo, and Gerald O'Driscoll.

# INTRODUCTION

Along with renewed interest in the Austrian school of economics over the last two decades, important advances have been made in applying its principles to concrete issues that typically face market economies. Several studies have appeared that analyze standard economic problems from an Austrian perspective. These include books in the areas of competition and monopoly (Armentano, 1990), monetary theory and policy (White, 1984 and Selgin, 1988), and industrial policy (Lavoie, 1985). In addition, since the late 1970's new works have been written which both clarify and extend various aspects of Austrian theory. Included in this list are books by Kirzner (1979) in which he extends his theories on entrepreneurship and the market process; O'Driscoll and Rizzo (1985) on the implications of time and uncertainty for economics; and collections of essays (Rizzo, ed., 1979; and Kirzner, ed., 1982) that include articles by Garrison, O'Driscoll, and Rothbard--among others--on such issues as the theories of capital, monopoly, and efficiency. Collectively, these analyses have had a significant impact on the direction and terms of discussion within the economics profession. The theories of entrepreneurship and competition, the analysis of banking institutions, and the economics of socialism have all been influenced by developments in modern Austrian economics.

In spite of this renewed interest, very little has been done in the area of externalities or, more generally, to develop an Austrian theory of welfare economics. Although Mises [1966 (1949)] and Rothbard (1962) have made modest attempts at presenting a positive theory of external effects, and Rothbard (1977) and Kirzner (1963, 1973, 1988A) have presented alternative theories of welfare economics most of the literature has been a reaction to, and criticism of, more orthodox approaches to these issues.

The overarching purpose of this book is to establish a sound theoretical basis for further empirical and public policy analysis in the area of externalities. In order to do this though, a general theory of welfare economics is required. Consequently, in chapter three, an alternative notion of efficiency is developed with implications that reach beyond the confines of externalities analysis.[1] The point to be made here is that, while the narrow focus of this book is on the economics of external effects, my more general purpose is to offer an alternative view of welfare economics--one that is divorced from perfect competition or any notion of general equilibrium.

Acting as a catalyst for the approach taken here are a host of theoretical and practical problems (discussed below) with standard welfare economics and its implications for the theory of externalities. These criticisms have been identified and brought to light most forcefully by scholars typically associated with the

Austrian school of economics.[2] Apart from this introduction, though, we do not dwell upon the problems associated with standard theory. Instead, an alternative framework of analysis is presented that takes seriously the very damaging criticism that Austrian economists have made. Hopefully, this alternative will be attractive to both Austrian and non-Austrian economists, who are uncomfortable with the received doctrine in this area.

## NEOCLASSICAL EXTERNALITIES THEORY

The concept of externalities was first discussed explicitly by Alfred Marshall in his Principles of Economics (1890). Here he introduced the familiar notions of external economies and diseconomies of scale or what Jacob Viner (1932) later called pecuniary externalities. But as Mishan has pointed out "[l]ittle attention was given to this concept until Pigou's celebrated *Economics of Welfare* . . . where it appears as one of the chief causes of divergences between 'private net product' and 'social net product'" (1971, p. 1). It is this analysis that gives rise to the normative conclusion that market activities which generate positive or negative effects will lead to less than optimal results in terms of prices charged and outputs produced.

The optimal solution is given by the price and output that is obtained under conditions that would exist in a perfectly competitive general equilibrium (PCGE). In this world marginal social benefit, given by price, equals marginal social cost, given by the monetary value of resource costs, in all markets. This result is shown to be Pareto optimal, i.e., no one can be made better off without making someone else worse off, and social efficiency is maximized. Externalities result in a deviation from this standard. A widely accepted definition of the term externality is given by Baumol and Oates:

> An externality is present whenever some individual's (say A's) utility or production relationships include real (that is nonmonetary) variables, whose values are chosen by others (persons, corporations, governments) without particular attention to the effects on A's welfare.[3] (Baumol and Oates, 1975, p. 17)

In other words an externality is any activity of B's that enters directly, but unintentionally, into A's production or utility function (Mishan, 1971).[4] A negative externality represents a cost that is not taken into consideration when output decisions are being made. Consequently, the resulting output level is greater than the Pareto optimal amount that would result in a PCGE and the market price is less than marginal social cost. Conversely, the generation of positive externalities gives rise to a level of output that is less than Pareto optimal since the market price is not capturing all of the benefits being generated from the production activity. Mishan states the standard conclusions as follows:

> . . . the equilibrium output of a competitive industry which generates an external diseconomy . . . is in excess of its optimal output. If positive, the optimal output is that at which the market price, less the social value of the marginal external diseconomy, is equal to the marginal resource cost. Conversely, if the competitive industry generates an external economy . . . its equilibrium output is below the optimal output obtained by equating to its marginal resource cost the market price plus the social value of the marginal external economy. (Mishan, 1971, p. 7)

In formulating policy remedies in this area policy makers and theorists attempt to induce the market to conform to the optimal results through the imposition of taxes or the provision of subsidies. For example, with respect to negative externalities an "appropriate" policy would be to impose an "excise tax [that] is equal to the value of the marginal external diseconomy at the optimal output" (Mishan, p. 7). This would force the generator of the externality to take into account all social costs associated with his production process, resulting in the optimal output being produced. Unlike excise taxes in general, such taxes, when calculated accurately, are said to correct for market failure and therefore enhance efficiency. According to Wallace Oates:

> The primary function of such taxes is to make the economy function more efficiently. Through their use we have the opportunity to employ the tax system, not only to raise revenues but also to enhance the operations of the economy. (Oates, 1988, p. 254)

With respect to goods that generate positive externalities, the same general logic is used in support of "an excise subsidy" to producers. Such subsidies should be "equal to the value of the marginal external economy" (Mishan, p. 7). This subsidy would allow the producer to realize all of the benefits associated with production of the good in question, ensuring that the optimal quantity is produced. In the extreme, potential external benefits in the provision of some good can result in the good not being produced at all. This would be that case of a "pure public good" (Samuelson, 1954), where once the good is produced it is equally available to all consumers and the consumption of it by one consumer does not reduce the amount of it available to others. In this case a severe "free rider problem" is expected to develop reducing effective demand for the product to zero. The policy conclusion here extends the excise subsidy to encompass the entire market output. It is necessary for the optimal quantity of the good to be produced by, or to have its production completely subsidized by, the government.

It is important to emphasize that the term optimal here refers to the result that is obtained in a PCGE. The value laden terms "over" and "under" production derive their normative significance from this definition of optimality. Austrian economists have typically argued that the PCGE is conceptually flawed and, as such, is irrelevant and non-operational as a guide for real-world public policy. Consequently, the entire theoretical framework that supports the "under/over" production view of externalities is rejected (see Cordato 1989 and 1992).

## THE AUSTRIAN CRITIQUE

There are several objections Austrian economists have typically raised to the standard neoclassical approach. These objections all center on certain tenets that are believed to be essential to economics, but are often ignored in traditional neoclassical analysis. These tenets can be categorized as follows: 1) market activity should be analyzed as a dynamic, disequilibrium process; 2) the concepts of value and utility are strictly subjective and therefore unobservable and unmeasurable (radical subjectivism); 3) knowledge of market phenomena, by both market participants and policymakers, is always imperfect.

These categories are not completely separable. In fact, full acceptance of any one of them requires an acceptance of the other two. For example, the principle that all costs and benefits are subjective and unmeasurable, implies that demand curves and cost curves cannot be known with certainty. If uncertainty exists, then errors in forecasting will be made both by consumers and entrepreneurs, implying that markets are not fully equilibrated. These major tenets have been invoked, both separately and in combination, in making some fundamental criticisms of the orthodox approach to welfare economics and its application in the area of externalities.

Austrian economists have been critical of many of the essential aspects of the standard analysis. In particular, they have rejected both the perfectly competitive model as a relevant welfare standard and by implication the normative analysis and policy conclusions derived from it. These criticisms have led Austrian school economists to the charge that the model is a non-operational standard for real world normative analysis.[5]

The most prominent criticism stems from the importance placed on the relationship between market activity and the passage of time. A standard assumption of welfare economics is that the market data, i.e. preferences, opportunity costs, relative scarcities, and technologies, is unchanging. Under such conditions the PCGE solution is also stable. But this is not the world that policy makers or market participants face. With the passage of time comes continuous changes in knowledge and therefore cost and preference functions. This view of markets has been emphasized by Ludwig Lachmann:

> As soon as we permit time to elapse, we must permit knowledge to change . . . The state of knowledge of society cannot be the same at two successive point of time, and time cannot elapse without demand and supply shifting. The stream of knowledge produces ever new disequilibrium situations, and entrepreneurs continually manage to find new price cost differences to exploit. (Lachmann, 1976, p. 128)

This is a perspective of the market process that is essentially open-ended (see Kirzner, 1988B), where adjustments to change are continuous--never reaching a conclusion or state of rest. In light of this, the extent to which the real world resembles a static (i.e., timeless) Pareto optimum cannot be a meaningful measure of performance for actual market processes. The implication is that even if a PCGE and therefore Pareto optimal market outcomes could be identified for a point in time (it will be argued below that this is an impossibility) they would immediately become obsolete as soon as time is allowed to pass.

By abstracting from the passage of time and by focussing on a perfectly competitive end state, the orthodox welfare standard judges market phenomena using a model of the world in which many of the most important elements of real markets are defined out of existence. Methodologically this is wholly illegitimate. O'Driscoll and Rizzo state the objection in the following manner:

> The received theory of competition is comparative static, focusing on beginning and end points. Economic agents are interested in neither the beginning nor the end points, but in coping with never ending adjustments. The theory of perfect competition analyzes the state of affairs or equilibrium conditions that would exist if all competitive activity ceased. **It is not an approximation but the negation of that activity.**
>
> All theories abstract from part of reality. Theorists must determine the appropriate degree of abstraction. What is essential and permanent to the phenomena ought to be part of the analysis. It would, for example, be pretty poor economic theory that abstracted from scarcity. All genuinely economic, as opposed to purely computational, problems arise, however, because of the passage of time and the concomitant changes in knowledge and the data. Economics must analyze the process of adaptation to change as surely as it analyzes scarcity. (O'Driscoll and Rizzo, p. 98, emphasis is in the original)

In the standard analysis, the welfare consequences of externalities are arrived at strictly by comparing the static equilibrium results that are obtained in the presence of externalities, ceteris paribus, with the Pareto optimum that is reached in the PCGE. But when markets are viewed as a dynamic, open-ended process this comparison becomes irrelevant for normative assessments of the real world. By implication, the public policy prescriptions that are derived from this comparison are equally irrelevant.

As is observed in Chapter 1, most Austrian economists have implicitly defined externalities as problematical only to the extent that they hinder "real world" market processes, i.e., to the extent that they prevent markets from taking account of information concerning scarcities and intrapersonally determined consumer and producer preferences (see Hayek quotation in note 8). In standard welfare economics the policy goal is to force the real world to mimic a PCGE. But this is a wholly unrealistic, and as will be argued below, conceptually meaningless welfare standard. Not only is this end state impossible to achieve in the real world, but, as will be noted below, it is empirically impossible to identify. With such identification impossible it can never be demonstrated that any particular policy is moving efficiency in a positive direction.

It should be pointed out that the issue of whether or not externalities give rise to a discrepancy between price and marginal social benefit or cost is not central to the dispute. Although, as will be discussed below, subjective value theory does imply some conceptual problems with this kind of terminology, what is being argued is that these discrepancies only have normative significance within the context of the standard equilibrium framework (Buchanan, 1969, pp. 40-41). If this framework is rejected then the normative significance of these discrepancies disappears.

A second criticism typically made by Austrian economists is derived from their strict adherence to subjective value theory. This criticism has important implications for the kind of information that is and isn't knowable by outside observers of the market process. In order to implement Pareto optimality as a welfare criteria, an analyst must make both interpersonal and intertemporal comparisons of costs and benefits, i.e., utility. For example, in order to identify any Pareto optimal state for a point in time, which must be done in order to determine whether some existing state is sub-optimal, utility, costs, and production functions must be specifiable. With specific regard to externalities, these functions must be known in order to show that the presence of an externality, by comparison to some Pareto optimum, creates conditions that can be improved upon. In order to theoretically or empirically demonstrate this suboptimal arrangement, interpersonal and intertemporal comparisons of costs and benefits must be made.

Any alteration of existing market conditions implies the transfer of resources among individuals. In order to show that social welfare, in the orthodox sense, is improved by transferring to B the use of resources that are currently being used by A, comparisons of marginal costs and benefits must be made across the two individuals. Since change can only take place through time, this comparison must also be made intertemporally. This automatically makes the standard welfare criteria impossible to implement. Buchanan has concisely stated the subjectivist view of costs, and, by implication, benefits.

> Cost is that which the decision-maker sacrifices or gives up when he selects one alternative rather than another. Cost consists therefore in his own evaluation of the enjoyment or utility that he anticipated having to

> forego as a result of choice itself . . . Cost is subjective; it exists only in the mind of the decision-maker or chooser . . . Cost cannot be measured by someone other than the chooser since there is no way that subjective mental experience can be directly observed. (Buchanan, 1981, pp. 14-15)[6]

These arguments can be extended to criticize the specific policy proposals that are put forth as standard solutions to externality problems. Implementing orthodox policy in this area in such a way as to effect a Pareto optimal solution involves calculating the social costs or benefits associated with the particular externality. But this type of calculus necessitates first measuring the externality-related costs or benefits for the affected individuals and then summing those results. But if one accepts Buchanan's description of the nature of costs (benefits), both of these steps are inherently impossible to carry out.

Buchanan applies the subjectivist approach to excise tax remedies for negative externality problems:

> Consider, first, the determination of the amount of the corrective tax that is to be imposed. This amount should equal the external costs that others than the decisionmaker suffer as a consequence of the decision. These costs are experienced by persons who may evaluate their own resultant utility losses . . . In order to estimate the size of the corrective tax, however, some objective measurement must be placed on these external costs. But the analyst has no benchmark from which plausible estimates can be made. Since the persons who bear these 'costs'--those who are externally affected--do not participate in the choice that generates the 'costs' there is simply no means of determining, even indirectly, the value that they place on the utility loss that might be avoided.[7] (Buchanan, 1969, p. 72)

The subjectivist approach calls into question the entire characterization of externalities as generating a divergence between private and social cost or benefits. All costs and benefits are inherently private. This does not mean that externalities do not impose costs or benefits on others, but to refer to them as "social" is a misnomer. As with all other costs and benefits, externalities are experienced subjectively, and cannot, either conceptually or practically, be added together to arrive at a measurement of "social" costs or benefits.

A third criticism of standard welfare economics and externalities analysis stems from what is typically referred to as the "knowledge problem." This issue was brought to light by Hayek in a series of articles on the nature of competitive market processes and rational calculation under socialism [1948 (1935A&B, 1945A&B)]. In recent years it has been applied to a number of other areas

(Boettke, 1990; Lavoie, 1985; Kirzner, 1985) including the tax-subsidy remedy to externality problems (O'Driscoll and Rizzo).

As has already been pointed out, both the passage of time and the subjective nature of costs and benefits, taken by themselves, create insurmountable obstacles to gaining the necessary information for implementing standard policy. But the "knowledge problem" arises even if one were to assume away the passage of time and the measurement problems posed by subjective value. The idea behind this stems from the complexity of the information requirements, even in a static setting. As has been emphasized, the standard policy is an attempt to impose a PCGE solution on a market or system of markets that is falling short of that solution. In order to do this the analyst must be able to gain knowledge of what the equilibrium solution is. Hayek has argued that this information is, by its very nature, highly decentralized and dispersed among individual market participants. He states that:

> . . . 'data' from which the economic calculus starts are never for the whole society 'given' to a single mind which could work out the implications and can never be so given.
>
> The peculiar character of the problem of a rational economic order is determined precisely by the fact that the knowledge of the circumstances of which we must make use never exists in concentrated or integrated form but solely as the dispersed bits of incomplete and frequently contradictory knowledge which all the separate individuals possess. [1948 (1945A), p. 77]

It is the task, then, of the market process itself to make use of this scattered knowledge; to bring it to bear on the production and consumption activities of people whose lives may be quite remote from those whose activities are generating the information. It does this through signals that are continuously sent by the price system. It is the responses to these continuously changing price signals, and the profits and losses they generate, that ensure that this information is utilized in market activities.[8]

The point made by Hayek is that no single mind or authority can obtain or keep current with the information embedded in actual market processes. In fact it is seen as one of the virtues of the market economy that it can continuously bring to light new information that could not possibly be gathered and disseminated in a centralized manner. With respect to externalities, in order for the standard tax or subsidy solution to work, the analyst must have better information concerning market conditions than is actually being generated in the markets themselves. If this were possible, the actual markets, and in particular the exchange relationships that comprise them, would not be needed. As O'Driscoll and Rizzo have argued:

> To know whether . . . [a market] process is optimal, we would need to know the very information whose discovery is the object of that process . . . [I]f we could independently ascertain the information, the . . . process would be superfluous. (p. 110)

It should be pointed out that this point does not go unrecognized by orthodox welfare economics. Allan Kneese, a consistent and articulate advocate of Pigouvian taxes as a remedy for negative externality problems, notes the problem succinctly:

> The general equilibrium model of resource allocation which underlies formal welfare economics represents . . . a general analysis of the interrelationships of markets throughout the economy. Because in principle it requires knowledge of the structure of preferences of all consumers and the technologies available to all producers, there is no realistic hope of ever being able to state the whole system empirically. (Kneese, 1977, p. 57)

Kneese's solution, which is the standard solution, to this problem is, in reality, to ignore it--that is, to revert to partial equilibrium analysis. According to Kneese, "in actual application small parts of the general system are extracted for detailed analysis" (1977, p. 57). This ignores the fact, highlighted by the theory of second best (R. E. Lipsey and K. J. Lancaster, 1957), that any optimal tax or subsidy is only optimal within the context of a general equilibrium solution. To derive the optimal tax or subsidy from the perspective of partial equilibrium analysis, one would have to know how it fits into the pattern of resource use in a world that is fully equilibrated. Partial equilibrium analysis ultimately must collapse into general equilibrium analysis.

As noted above, even if the complex information requirements necessary to identify a Pareto optimal solution could be met for a particular point in time, the passage of time implies changes in that solution. The problem, then, is one of centralizing, and then keeping current with all of the information necessary for determining both the equilibrium solution for any single point in time and all relevant future points. Before the data could be gathered and the optimal tax or subsidy could be calculated, the information would be outdated. This problem alone would prevent any tax or subsidy that is implemented from ever being "optimal" (O'Driscoll and Rizzo, p. 140).

O'Driscoll and Rizzo have likened this whole series of issues regarding tax policy to those that were raised by Mises [1981 (1922)] and Hayek as part of their critique of socialist planning schemes. Mises and Hayek argued that resources could not be allocated efficiently in a centrally planned system for essentially the same reasons that we have been discussing. That is, the information that is necessary for efficient resource allocation cannot be known to any central authority. With respect to both socialism and externalities analysis, it is the possibility of efficient non-market resource allocation that is being called into question. As O'Driscoll and Rizzo have pointed out:

> In the Mises-Hayek analysis, socialism is intervention carried out systematically in all markets. It substitutes non-price and non-market allocations for pricing and market institutions. Particularistic intervention at the micro-level is socialism writ small . . . Consider the use of taxes to influence output levels . . . If a tax rate is to be optimal, policy makers must know the optimal level of the taxed activity (e.g. discharging effluents into a river) . . . [T]he informational requirements for [optimal taxation] are simply those for optimal non-price resource allocation. There can be no theory of optimal . . . taxing behavior until there is a theory of non-price resource allocation that actually addresses the original Mises-Hayek argument.[9] (O'Driscoll and Rizzo, p. 141)

The Austrian criticisms of the standard approach to externalities are fundamental. For this reason, any Austrian alternative must entail more than simply marginal adjustments to the orthodox approach. There needs to be a reconstruction of welfare economics, in addition to drawing out its implications for the normative effects of externalities.

## OUTLINE AND ORGANIZATIONAL FRAMEWORK

The orthodox analysis of externalities involves three essential levels: a theory of welfare economics, a normative interpretation of externalities in light of that theory, and a discussion of policy remedies. The theory presented here is similarly organized. The book has six chapters. Chapter 1, "The Genealogy of the Austrian Approach," examines the conclusions that Austrian economists have typically reached with respect to the welfare effects of externalities. The discussion here highlights the important differences that have developed between Austrian and more traditional neoclassical economists. With the notable exception of Hayek, Austrian school economists have taken the position that only external effects involving the conflicting use of property prevent a market from reaching its potential in terms of social welfare. This analysis is found most explicitly in the works of Mises (1966) and Rothbard (1962), but its roots can be traced to the writings of the early Austrians, particularly Menger, Böhm-Bawerk, and Wieser.

Austrian economists have rejected the standard neoclassical approach to welfare economics, but no single Austrian theory of welfare economics has emerged to take its place. Chapter 2 critically examines some concepts of welfare economics that have been developed by Austrian school economists. In particular, the theories introduced by Kirzner (1963, 1973, 1988A) and Rothbard

(1977) are evaluated in light of their ability to provide a normative grounding for externalities analysis. In Chapter 3 an alternative theory of efficiency is built in light of problems that face these previous attempts. This alternative theory makes use of the distinction that Mises (1966) and Hayek (1976) have drawn between "economy" and "catallaxy." Traditionally economists have analyzed markets and discussed public policy in terms of "economic" efficiency. But when markets are viewed as an open-ended disequilibrium process it becomes clear that the concept of economic efficiency is inappropriate. What we typically call an economy is more accurately described as a catallaxy. In chapter 3 we develop a theory of "catallactic efficiency" which takes into consideration this more accurate description of the market process.

Chapters 4 and 5 specifically deal with the issue of externalities from the perspective of catallactic efficiency. Chapter 4 reexamines the externality problem in light of the alternative perspective on efficiency and compares these conclusions with the more traditional Pigouvian approach. Chapter 5 further develops this contrast by applying the normative theory of externalities developed in the previous chapter to the economic analysis of tort law. In this area a clear distinction can be seen between the property rights analysis that was introduced by Coase and later developed by Posner, among others, and the property rights analysis of the Austrians.

Clearly, all of the issues surrounding the question of externalities cannot be resolved in one volume. The purpose here is to establish a framework of analysis for further research. The concluding chapter suggests some important areas where further theoretical and practical analysis needs to be done. Two important theoretical issues left unanswered relate to the role of economics in establishing property rights to unowned resources, and to the question of whether externalities theory gives an economic rationalization for the existence of government. Some practical issues that are left unresolved concern the problems of identification and large numbers that plague all economic analysis of certain kinds of pollution problems. Furthermore, it is important to ask whether there is room for a notion of "second best" within the context of Austrian analysis in resolving practical problems that might arise. This concluding chapter attempts to clarify some of the issues that need to be dealt with in order to eventually give satisfactory answers to these questions.

## NOTES

1 As Professor Armentano discusses in his "Forward" to this book, the notion of "catallactic efficiency" has some important implications as a normative standard in the other general area of welfare economics, competition and monopoly.

2 This is referred to as the Austrian school because its late 19th century founders (primarily Menger, Wieser, and Böhm-Bawerk) and their students (most notably Mises and his student, Hayek) originally studied and practiced economics in Vienna. Most contemporary Austrian economists are located in the United States.

3 This definition is widely endorsed. See Buchanan and Stubblebine (1962) and Mishan (1971).

4 The common mathematical representation is $F^1(x_1^{\ 1}, x_1^{\ 2}, \ldots, x_1^{\ m}, x_2^{\ n})$. $F_1$ is the utility level of person 1 and the x's are the amounts of goods $X^1$, $X^2$, etc., that are being consumed by person 1. $x_2^{\ n}$ is the amount of some good $X^n$ that is being consumed (produced) by individual 2. In this case individual 1's utility level depends directly upon individual 2's consumption (production) of $X^n$ (Mishan, 1971).

5 For criticisms of its use as a guide to antitrust policy see Armentano (1990). For more general criticisms see Hayek (1948), or O'Driscoll and Rizzo (1985).

6 For a more complete criticism of both standard welfare economics and utility theory, from a strictly subjectivist perspective, see Rothbard (1977).

7 William Baumol, a consistent supporter of the tax-subsidy approach in this area, has admitted Buchanan's point stating that:

> . . . one must concede . . . that objective cost data do not enable us to calculate the ideal Pigouvian tax-subsidy figures to deal with externalities . . . (Baumol, 1970, p. 1211)

In spite of his recognition of this point, he concludes in favor of the Pigouvian approach:

> it seems to me that the general approach, utilized in full consciousness of the imperfection of our information, still offers us the most promising means available to

> regulate many of our externalities problems. (Baumol, 1970, p. 1211)

8 Hayek sees this as the primary economic problem facing a society. He argues that:

> The economic problem of society is thus not merely a problem of how to allocate 'given' resources . . . It is rather a problem of how to secure the best use of resources known to any of the members of society, for ends whose relative importance only these individuals know. Or, to put it briefly, it is a problem of the utilization of knowledge which is not given to anyone in its totality. [1948 (1945A), pp. 77-78]

9 It is sometimes argued that a tax-subsidy approach, as opposed to a regulatory approach, to externality problems is a market remedy (Stroup and Baden, 1983). O'Driscoll and Rizzo dispute this, arguing that:

> The informational requirements of taxation and regulatory approaches are formally identical . . . And the informational requirements for optimal regulation are simply those for optimal nonprice resource allocation . . .
>
> Taxation of an activity is often proffered as a 'market' approach, which substitutes for a regulatory or interventionist approach. Economists mislead themselves and their readers[]by speaking of 'tax prices.' The only shared feature that taxes have with prices is their dimensionality. Taxes do not result from a market process, nor do they reflect allocational decisions of resource owners . . . In other words, taxation is a method of intervening, not an alternative to intervention or nonmarket allocation. (O'Driscoll and Rizzo, p. 141-142)

# 1

## THE GENEALOGY OF THE AUSTRIAN POSITION

In casually surveying the analysis of externality questions among modern Austrian economists one is struck with the fact that most discussions center around externality problems involving conflicts in the use of property, such as pollution. On the other hand, very little is written about the consequences of other external effects such as free-rider or public goods problems. This narrow focus does not arise from any oversight on the part of Austrian writers. It results from a distinctly Austrian perspective on the question of externalities, which, in turn arises from a refusal to view welfare economics in terms of perfectly competitive market outcomes. Typically it has been argued that only those externalities involving a conflict in the use of property will have negative effects on the workings of a market economy. Consequently, the only policy relevant externalities are those that arise because of property rights that are not clearly defined or strictly enforced. In direct contrast, Pigouvian analysis concludes that all non-pecuniary externalities are evidence of market failure, i.e., have negative effects on social welfare, and that all externality problems are at least potentially policy relevant.

This chapter concentrates on the theoretical and normative distinctions that most Austrians have made between different types externalities. No attempt is made here to provide a welfare economics justification for the Austrian school position as it has developed. (This issue is reserved for chapters 2 and 3.) Neither of the two most important figures in the development of this view, Mises and Rothbard, explicitly based their assessment of externalities on a clearly defined theory of economic welfare, although in a separate context Rothbard has elaborated an alternative approach to welfare economics (1977). On the other hand, most of the views discussed in this chapter can be interpreted as simply the result of rejecting the perfectly competitive general equilibrium as a benchmark for normative analysis.

The discussion proceeds as follows. First there is a review of the predominant Austrian attitude toward the issues of negative and positive externalities as represented in the writings of Mises and Rothbard. The Mises-Rothbard approach has clearly had the most influence among Austrian economists in general. As is pointed out below, Hayek's position on the question of external benefits is essentially different from that of other modern Austrians. His view is analyzed separately. To obtain a better understanding of the Mises-Rothbard position we will examine the views of those early Austrian economists whose writings are relevant to this issue; primarily Menger, Böhm-Bawerk, and to a lesser extent, Wieser. Clearly there are elements of the more modern position in the writings of the Austrian school's founders.

## MISES AND ROTHBARD ON EXTERNALITIES

### Negative Externalities

> "The problem of 'external costs' . . . is a consequence of failure to enforce fully the rights of property . . . Hence external costs (e.g., smoke damage) are failures to maintain a fully free market, rather than defects of that market." (Rothbard, 1962, p. 944)

The notion that policy-relevant negative externalities are exogenous to, rather than an endogenous part of a market economy, is clearly the most distinctive aspect of the Austrian approach to the question of external costs. Both Mises and Rothbard, the two most notable Austrian economists to explicitly define what is meant by an external cost, are clear in linking them directly to the use of property. According to both authors the clear definition and strict enforcement of property rights are essential for the functioning of a market economy. It is concluded, therefore, that any problems associated with what are usually called negative externalities such as air, water, and noise pollution, result from the failure of those legal institutions charged with defining and enforcing property rights and not with the market system itself. For example, Mises argued that all negative externality problems "could be removed by a reform of the laws concerning liability for damages inflicted and by rescinding the institutional barriers preventing the full operation of private ownership" (1966, p. 658). As will be noted below, to the extent that any problems can be associated with positive external effects, there resolution is to be found in similar property rights solutions.

This is not to argue that negative externalities do not cause problems for a market economy which are similar to those discussed in Pigouvian welfare economics. Both specific prices and the economic calculation based on them will be altered in the presence of negative externalities. Mises called these altered prices "deceptive" (1966, p. 658) and pointed out that "some people choose certain modes of want satisfaction merely on account of the fact that a part of the costs incurred are debited not to them but to other people" (1966, p. 656). What is absent from this discussion (and from Rothbard's) is any reference to an optimal price/output combination that the free market "fails" to produce. This stems from their rejection of the static state of Pareto optimality as a normative benchmark for economic analysis. Problems that arise from external costs do show evidence that the economic system is "failing." This failure, though, is due to the fact that certain aspects of the system are not consistent with free markets, rather than because they are. If the necessary institutional conditions for a free market process are not present then the market cannot be blamed for the outcome. For Mises and Rothbard these conditions include both clearly defined and strictly enforced property rights.

The view that negative externality problems are not the result of market failure but are the result of the circumvention of markets continues to be emphasized in the more recent contributions to the Austrian literature. Rizzo and O'Driscoll blame the presence of external costs on the "absence of markets and improperly specified property rights" (p. 142). And they suggest that the associated problems should be solved in the way property rights disputes are typically solved, through the courts.

Much of this can be explained by the traditional Austrian emphasis on dynamic market processes. What makes a free market process desirable is that it gives rise to prices and outputs that reflect the ongoing allocational decisions of resource owners, not that it results in a Pareto optimal, general equilibrium end state. For Mises and Rothbard negative externalities result in resources being allocated by non-owners, either because ownership rights are not being enforced or because they are not clearly defined.

This raises some questions about externalities that do not involve the conflicting use of property. For example, what if neighbor A keeps junk cars in his back yard and neighbor B considers this unsightly? How would this be viewed from the Mises/Rothbard perspective? Although this type of situation is not addressed directly, the implication is that it is not one that could be improved upon by means other than voluntary market exchange. Mises and Rothbard both concluded that a market system will function as beneficially as possible when the institutional setting is such that all rights to property are clearly defined and strictly enforced (Mises, 1978, pp. 52-59 & 1966, p. 655; Rothbard 1962, chapter 12).

In the example above, even though A may be imposing some psychic costs on B, considering the implications of subjective value theory, there would be no way to unambiguously improve upon these results through a non-voluntary rearrangement of property rights. Since the satisfaction levels of A and B cannot be observed or measured it would be meaningless for any outside observer to compare A's utility losses to B's utility gains. In fact, there would be no way to discern even whether the externality exists.[1] On the other hand, a solution reached voluntarily (within the property rights framework described above) to internalize these costs, such as side payments or the erection of a fence, would represent an unambiguous improvement in social welfare.

The point here is that both Mises and Rothbard describe institutional settings that they argue will allow markets to function as efficiently as possible. Part of this setting for both authors (see also Kirzner, 1963 p. 13) is that people be allowed to make all decisions with respect to the use of their own property. It is not argued that within this setting all negative externalities will be eliminated.

Instead it is clear that Mises and Rothbard would both conclude that this type of institutional setting would maximize the internalization of negative externalities. Like more traditional economic analysis of negative externalities (for an exception see Coase 1960), Austrians view internalization as welfare enhancing. When that internalization can be accomplished by enforcing or more clearly defining property rights, i.e., ensuring the institutional setting mentioned above, it will allow for a more efficiently operating market process. But in the example above, where rights are clearly defined and no one's property rights are being violated, only a voluntary agreement to internalize the externality would lead to an unambiguous improvement.

**External Benefits**

> The case of external economies is not simply the inversion of external costs. (Mises, 1966, p. 658)

> The problem of external costs, usually treated as symmetrical with external benefits, is not really related. (Rothbard, 1962, p. 944)

Positive externalities, for normative purposes, have typically been viewed quite differently from external costs. As both Mises and Rothbard suggest, the symmetry between the two that is typically found in standard welfare economics, i.e., that they both have a negative impact on social welfare, has not been part of the Austrian approach.[2] Since, generally, they do not involve conflicts in the use of property, external benefits per se are not viewed as evidence of either market or institutional failure. In fact, it can be argued that, in many respects, the welfare effects of external benefits are an unintended fringe benefit of a market system.

To reiterate, since most positive external effects are not typically associated with property rights that are either undefined or unenforced, they are not generally deemed problematical. But as will be noted below, Mises has identified certain instances, primarily with respect to inventions and publishing, where, he feels, adverse consequences for social welfare can be associated with positive external effects. But even here the issue is not a problem of external benefits per se but, again, a problem of clearly defining or more strictly enforcing property rights.

Once again among Austrian writers it is primarily Mises and Rothbard who address these issues on a general level, that is, not strictly in terms of particular cases such as education (High 1985), road congestion (Block, 1983), etc. Generally both Mises and Rothbard tend to view external benefits as worthy of discussion at all only because the economics profession has traditionally viewed the issue as important. Mises, for example, after giving only a simple two paragraph definition of external benefits out of his 900-page treatise, *Human Action*, concludes that:

> It would hardly be necessary to say more about external economies if it were not for the fact that this phenomenon is entirely misinterpreted in current [economic] literature. (Mises, 1966, p. 658)

With the elimination of the perfectly competitive end state as the normative benchmark, external benefits per se can be viewed, from a normative perspective, like any other kind of benefit. Since the term benefit under ordinary circumstances implies welfare enhancement, then in the absence of orthodox normative standards any external benefits actually generated would have to imply a gain in social welfare. Certainly there is no basis from which to argue that "not enough" of the good or service is being produced. Not enough compared to what?

On the level of positive analysis it is recognized that the presence of external benefits can be invoked to explain why particular goods or services may go unproduced, or why certain trades may not take place. Mises recognizes two possible outcomes given the presence of external benefits. Neither has special normative significance. For ease of reference they will be referred to as type 1 and type 2 external benefits.

> 1. The planning actor considers the advantages which he expects for himself so important that he is prepared to defray all the costs required. The fact that his project also benefits other people will not prevent himself from accomplishing what promotes his own well-being.
>
> 2. The costs incurred by a project are so great that none of those whom it will benefit is ready to expend them in full. (Mises, 1966, p. 658)

Neither of these results is viewed as a shortcoming of the market. Since the relevant standard of optimality is not the perfectly competitive world, there is no reason to conclude that the resulting price-quantity combination, in either case, is sub-optimal. These outcomes simply reflect the freely made decisions of market participants to trade or not to trade under one of an infinite number of cost-benefit relationships. In the absence of the perfectly competitive welfare standard, there is no reason to single these decisions out relative to others that might be made under different market circumstances.

In the first instance the good is produced in spite of the presence of external benefits. In the standard framework it would be argued that too little of the good is being produced, relative to the Pareto optimal outcome in a perfectly competitive general equilibrium (PCGE). Therefore the market has failed to allocate resources in a socially efficient manner. Austrian analysis of this same situation would argue quite differently. Since there is no optimal outcome apart from that which is generated by the actual interaction of market participants, there is no standard by which to argue that "too little" is being produced. Given this perspective, external benefits of this nature, rather than being viewed as evidence of market failure, are considered to be a fringe benefit of the market process.

Rothbard argues that the market process is filled with such external benefits, and that we all, in some way, benefit from them.

> . . . which one of us would earn anything like our present real income were it not for external benefits that we derive from the actions of others? Specifically, the great modern accumulation of capital goods is an inheritance from all the net savings of our ancestors . . . We are all, therefore, free riders on the past. We are also free riders on the present, because we benefit from the continuing investment of our fellow men and from their specialized skills on the market. (1962, p. 888)

Rothbard considers these, and all other external benefits that are actually realized as a result of the market process, to be welfare enhancing. Whether or not the generators of these externalities capture the marginal benefits associated with them has no normative significance in the absence of a PCGE welfare standard. The fact that Mises and Rothbard see all the effects of type 1 externalities as beneficial explains why no corrective policy is necessary. The second result associated with external benefits, i.e., where "the project can be realized only if a sufficient number of those interested in it share in the costs," is analogous to the standard public goods/free rider dilemma. The standard analysis suggests that if the good fails to get produced on the market, due to excessive transactions costs or a failure on the part of consumers to reveal their "true" preferences, then it is the proper role of government to provide such outputs. This is simply an extension of the argument usually made with respect to type 1 positive externalities, where the good will be provided, but in less than optimal quantities.

Mises generally views the results of this type of externality strictly as an explanation of why certain trades may not take place on an open market. Since these outcomes are consistent with preferences as they have been revealed through market behavior, they are not seen as a failure of the market system to allocate resources efficiently. In fact, Mises argues that it is the government's rearrangement of the market outcome that would have to result in the misallocation of resources. In response to the standard policy recommendations mentioned above, Mises argues that:

> the means which a government needs in order to run a plant . . . or to subsidize [a] project must be withdrawn either from the taxpayers' spending and investing power or from the loan market . . . Public works . . . are paid for by funds taken away from the citizens . . . the citizens would have employed them for the realization of profit promising projects . . . For every unprofitable project that is realized by the aid of

> the government there is a corresponding project the realization of which is neglected merely on account of the government's intervention. Yet this nonrealized project would have been profitable, i.e., it would have employed the scarce means of production in accordance with the most urgent needs of consumers. From the point of view of consumers the . . . unprofitable project is wasteful. (1966, p. 659)

As one analyst has pointed out, the standard approach to these types of external benefits "take[s] an explanation as to why certain trades do not take place and turn[s] this explanation into a normative statement that the trade should have taken place" (Brownstein, 1980). Given the Austrian view of markets and market processes, this approach is wholly illegitimate. There is no way for the economist or policy maker to know the preferences of market participants apart from what the individuals reveal them to be through action (Mises 1966, pp. 94-96). In an unhampered market, assuming clearly defined and strictly enforced property rights, prices and outputs will tend to reflect the preferences of market participants as revealed through decisions to make or not make certain exchanges. The existence of external benefits does not distort this tendency, even in the extreme case where the good is not produced. The standard argument is that good X will not be produced in the presence of an extensive free-rider problem. More specifically, even if the individuals making up the potential market for the good all will benefit from its production, none of those individuals will actually contract for X's provision, in hopes of receiving the good without bearing the costs. This is the "pure public goods" problem. For Mises and Rothbard the potential consumers of this product have revealed a preference not to pay an amount sufficient enough to induce its production. It is illegitimate for economists, qua economist, to normatively evaluate the motives behind this preference. The actors' value scales must be taken as given. To suggest that consumers really prefer something other than the market outcome is to substitute the values of the economist for the revealed values of market participants. (Rothbard, 1962, p. 890)

Mises' discussion diverges slightly from Rothbard's in that he notes certain problems that he feels can be associated with type 2 externality results that are the consequence of unclearly defined property. The most apparent expression of this is in the "'production' of the intellectual groundwork of every kind of processing and constructing" (Mises 1966, p. 661). Mises recognizes that the presence of excessive external economies may hinder new inventions and the publication of new ideas, and argues that these external economies could be internalized through a property rights solution, i.e., by instituting patents and copyrights. Although Mises explicitly refrains from directly endorsing patent and copyright laws (1966, p. 662) he does allow for the possibility that, at least in certain instances, the internalization of external benefits through a more clear definition of property rights may improve social welfare. He argues that "it is unlikely that people would undertake the laborious task of writing [needed textbooks, manuals, handbooks, and other nonfiction works] if everyone were free to reproduce them." Furthermore he argues that "the extensive experimentation necessary for [technological invention and discovery] is often very expensive." He concludes that "[i]t is very probable that technological progress would be seriously retarded if, for the inventor and for those who defray the expenses incurred by his experimentation, the results obtained were nothing but external economies" (1966, p. 662).

What should be noted is that to the extent Mises sees a problem arising with external benefits at all, he traces its roots to a more fundamental issue related to "the delimitation of property rights" (1966, p. 662). While Rothbard opposes patent and copyright laws, Mises' approach does not diverge from Rothbard's in a fundamental sense. The over-riding theme is consistent: to the extent that economics implies any corrective policy it is in the area of either more clearly defining or strictly enforcing property rights.

The difference between Mises and Rothbard on the issue of patents and copyrights can be found not in their approach to externalities as such, but in their approach to property rights. Rothbard uses as his criterion for defining property rights a Lockean natural-rights ethic. From his perspective, intellectual property rights cannot be derived from principles of natural law and therefore the state has no moral "right" to impose them through the institution of patent and copyright laws. To do so would, from Rothbard's perspective, violate property rights that already exist. He states that:

> . . . patents actually invade the property rights of those independent discoverers of an idea or an inventor who happen to make the discovery after the patentee . . . Patents, therefore invade rather than defend property rights (1970, p. 71).

Mises, on the other hand, rejects all natural law arguments for property rights (1978), adopting a strictly utilitarian approach. This allows him to be more flexible in considering alternative property rights arrangements. The underlying conclusion though, on the part of both authors, is that once property rights are clearly established a policy of strict laissez faire is seen as best promoting social welfare, even in the face of any external benefits or "free rider problems" that might still exist. Both Mises and Rothbard reject standard free rider justifications for either government subsidization or direct provision of any goods or services. Even though Mises is in favor of a minimal state apparatus to provide for the enforcement of property rights, there is no indication in his writings that the justification is based on free rider arguments.

### Concluding Remarks on Mises and Rothbard

As a result of this underlying view of the relationship between market efficiency and property rights the Mises/Rothbard position on externalities shows two dominant characteristics, one a derivation of the other. The first is in the area of welfare effects; the second is in the area of policy. First, only externalities involving either the conflicting use or unclear definition of property are necessarily inconsistent with the efficient functioning of a market process. The second characteristic, implied by the first, relates to economic policy. The presence of positive or negative external effects even in the extreme case of Mises' type 2 externality, is never a sufficient cause for government provision of a good or intervention into a market. Any problems associated with externalities must be the result of ambiguously defined or poorly enforced property rights before they can be considered the subject of policy.

These characteristics dominate the analysis of particular externality problems that is found in the modern Austrian literature. With respect to positive externality issues most of the analysis attempts to show why the presence of a particular external effect is not a sufficient justification for government intervention (High 1985, Block 1983). With respect to negative externalities, nearly all discussions tend to center on situations that involve direct conflicts in property usage, such as air and water pollution problems (Littlechild, 1979; Rizzo and O'Driscoll 1985; Rothbard 1982).

Because these conclusions regarding the welfare effects of externalities and public policy dominate the Austrian literature on externalities, they will be used as a reference point for subsequent analysis in this chapter. The relevant works of both the early Austrians and Hayek, whose analyses can be contrasted with this dominant view, will be assessed in light of the approach established by Mises and Rothbard.

## HAYEK ON EXTERNAL BENEFITS AND "COLLECTIVE GOODS"[3]

Hayek's perspective on this issue has emerged as the most notable exception to the Mises/Rothbard analysis. His conclusions with respect to external benefits and "collective goods" tend to be more consistent with neoclassical analysis than with the Mises/Rothbard approach outlined above, even though he explicitly rejects the welfare standards from which the orthodox conclusions are derived.

His analysis of collective goods focuses primarily on the divergence between costs incurred and benefits received rather than on conflicts in property usage. He first asserts that the "effectiveness of the market order . . . rests on the fact that in most instances the producers of particular goods and services will be able to determine who will benefit from them and who pay for their costs" (p. 43). He further argues that when externalities are present this is not completely possible. Hayek concludes that under these circumstances there will not be a "balance of costs and benefits" and "the conditions which the market requires in order to perform its ordering function" will not be completely satisfied (p. 43).

Unlike Mises and Rothbard, Hayek argues that the mere presence of external benefits threatens the efficient workings of a market process. From the observation that, due to extensive external benefits "it would be prohibitively costly to confine certain services to particular persons so that these services can be provided only for all" (p. 48), he concludes that "government may have to step in where the market fails to supply a needed service" (p. 49). In this classification, Hayek includes nearly all of the standard cases of public goods including defense, education, roads, and flood protection. He invokes the orthodox "free rider" argument, stating that:

> Where large numbers are involved, most individuals, no matter how much they may wish the services in question should be made available, will reasonably believe that it will make no difference to the results whether they themselves agree to contribute to the costs or not. Nor will any individual who consents to contribute have the assurance that the others will also do so . . . Indeed wholly rational considerations will lead each individual, while wishing that all the others would contribute, to refuse himself to do so . . . [C]ompulsion . . . will in many instances be the only way in which collective goods can be provided . . . (p. 44)

It is clear that Hayek diverges from the dominant Austrian position with respect to both characteristics outlined above. First positive externalities per se are viewed as impinging upon the efficient operation of the market process whether or not they are associated with poorly defined or enforced property rights. Consequently their presence is viewed, at least with respect to those collective goods he identifies, as a sufficient justification for government provision or subsidization. In addition these are not just pure public goods, or Mises' type 2 externality goods, but goods that would and do get produced in spite of the associated positive externalities. These include education, park services, quality certification of products and even maps (p. 44).

**Hayekian Analysis and Hayek on Externalities**

Hayek's discussions of externalities appears to be inconsistent with much of his own general framework of analysis in other areas. In the same volume where the discussions of collective goods are found, Hayek, in connection with another issue, makes the following statement:

> . . . the whole of the so-called 'welfare economics', which pretends to base its arguments on the inter-personal comparisons of ascertainable utilities, lacks all scientific foundation. The fact that most of us believe

> that they can judge which of the several needs of two or more known persons are more important, does not prove either that there is any objective basis for this, nor [sic] that we can form such a conceptions[sic] about people whom we do not know individually. The idea of basing coercive actions by government on such fantasies is clearly an absurdity. (pp 201-202)

This statement, which invokes a subjectivist approach to questions of policy analysis consistent with that taken by Mises and Rothbard, cannot be reconciled with Hayek's analysis of the free rider problem and collective goods. On the one hand he rejects the welfare standard used in neoclassical externalities analysis but embraces much of the analysis that is derived from it. His assessment of welfare economics leaves little room for the policy prescriptions that he suggests are appropriate.

In his analysis of collective goods Hayek argues that a person really desires a trade and therefore should be compelled to make it when in fact that person has assessed the market and has decided to abstain from participation. Given his own perspective on welfare economics and subjective value, Hayek's judgment concerning the person's true preference cannot be a scientifically made. The fact that the abstention may be due to free rider considerations should not, in and of itself, make a difference. Given Hayek's rejection of neoclassical welfare economics, it is not evident how he differentiates, for normative consideration, a free rider rationale for refusing to carry out a trade from any other reason for not entering into a market transaction. Hayek freely accepts the implications of rejecting the standard welfare analysis in the area of competition and monopoly, for example, but there is no evidence that he fully recognizes them in the other major area of the market failure literature, externalities analysis.

There are other aspects of Hayek's general framework that are at odds with his assessment of the externalities question. The knowledge problem that plays such an important role in Hayek's analysis of economic calculation under socialism [1948 (1935A&B, and 1945B)] and the nature of the competitive market process [(1948, (1945A)] goes unrecognized when he analyzes this issue. Hayek assumes that the authorities can know which goods are not being produced due to excessive external benefits and which goods fail to be produced because of other, non-externality related cost considerations. But given the knowledge problems which Hayek suggests are relevant with respect to nearly all other areas of government intervention, this would be impossible to determine. In Hayek's own words:

> To use a standard by which we measure the actual achievement of competition the hypothetical arrangements made by an omniscient dictator comes naturally to the economist whose analysis must proceed on the fictitious assumption that he knows all the facts which determine the order of the market. But it does not provide us with a valid test

> which can meaningfully be applied to the achievements of practical policy (p. 67).

Yet Hayek himself seems to fall into this trap. Conceptually, it can be argued that there will be goods that the market will not produce because of excessive external benefits. But Hayek claims to know what many of these goods actually are and proceeds to list them. It would appear that he is playing the part of the economist he criticizes.

A related issue concerns Hayek's assertion, when discussing externalities, that "the effectiveness of the market order" depends on the ability of market participants to identify who will benefit and who will bear the costs of market activity. The fact that this is true to some extent cannot be denied. For example, in order for a business to be successful it must be able to identify a market for its product and be able to identify the costs incurred by different aspects of its operation. But to state this relationship in an unqualified manner is inconsistent with Hayek's own emphasis on the beneficial, unintended consequences that he considers essential in generating a market order. Hayek regularly points out that market activity always generates unintended benefits that are not and never could be known fully by the market participants who are generating them. Hayek states that:

> It is because in the catallaxy men, while following their own interests, whether wholly egotistical or highly altruistic, will further the aims of many others, most of whom they will never know, that it is an overall order so superior to any deliberate organization . . . (1976, p. 110)

The only aspect of Hayek's analysis where knowledge problems associated with externalities seem to be considered is in the actual provision of collective goods. Hayek argues that while the state should provide certain goods or at least subsidize their production, it should not seize or grant monopoly privileges in this process. Recognizing that new technology could transform a public good into a private good, Hayek states that:

> Even if in given circumstances only government is in fact able to supply particular services, this is no reason for prohibiting private agencies from trying to find methods of providing these services without the use of coercive powers . . . New methods may be found for making a service saleable which before could not be restricted to those willing to pay for it, and thus make the market method applicable to areas where before it could not be applied. (p. 47)

Here Hayek recognizes that new knowledge could come to bear on the provision of certain collective goods, making it possible to internalize the external benefits. By allowing private firms to compete with the state, the profit motive will encourage the discovery of any new techniques.

Typically, Hayek is also critical of policy prescriptions that are based on states of affairs "that might have been achieved if certain facts which we cannot alter were other that [sic] they in fact are" (p. 67). Yet this is precisely the case with "collective goods." Because of certain cost considerations facing potential participants in certain markets, namely the cost of organizing markets in the face of extensive free riders, the goods that would otherwise be produced are not. Hayek would have little concern if this result were due to excessive transportation or labor costs. Furthermore, he gives no indication as to why this particular type of cost, i.e., a transactions cost, should be viewed differently. The "collective goods" scenario is consistent with the actual costs that are faced by market participants. If the cost constraints were different, then the results would be different. In the framework of the perfectly competitive model, transactions costs are singled out because they are inconsistent with a perfectly competitive, Pareto optimal outcome. Hayek rejects this welfare standard but offers no alternative justification for normatively evaluating transactions costs differently from other costs. From Hayek's own perspective, it is not clear how he can legitimately advocate economic policies which attempt to impose outcomes that would have occurred if only actual market conditions had been different.

While Hayekian analysis has traditionally been a beacon for modern Austrian economic analysis, his assessment of the externalities issue is clearly inconsistent with many of his own analytical precepts. Clear evidence of this is that other Austrian economists have not followed Hayek's lead when analyzing externality problems.

## EXTERNALITIES ANALYSIS AND THE EARLY AUSTRIANS

Self-conscious externalities analysis in economics did not come into being until after the 1920's and the publication of Pigou's *Economics of Welfare* (1954, first ed. 1920). For this reason, any observations with respect to the views of the early Austrian writers on this subject must involve a healthy dose of both conjecture and inference. In spite of this, it is possible to trace some of the roots of Mises' and Rothbard's approach to externalities to the writings of the school's founders, Menger, Böhm-Bawerk, and Wieser.

### Carl Menger

In Menger's writing, discussions of specific kinds of externalities appear in the analysis of certain social and economic processes. The approach that Menger takes when assessing these specific external effects is remarkably similar to the approach taken by latter-day Austrians. It is clear that Menger saw the existence of negative externalities that involve the conflicting use of property as a problem that an economic system would need to resolve. On the other hand, Menger views external benefits that are generated within the context of clearly defined property rights as having only positive consequences.

Although the terms "externality," "external costs" or "external benefits" were not part of the 19th century economist's vocabulary, Menger does recognize the issue when discussing problems that arise from the conflicting use of property. He argues that because goods are scarce and people's preferences diverge, different plans with respect to particular units of property will come into conflict. He uses the presence of these conflicts as an explanation for the emergence of the institution of private property. In both Mises and Rothbard, conflicting goals with respect to the use of property is at the heart of problems created by externalities. While they, and other modern Austrians use the existence of these conflicts to derive normative conclusions (i.e., an efficient market process dictates that property rights be defined and enforced) Menger's motives were primarily positive.

He used the reality of conflicting property usage to explain the observable phenomenon of private property. In the process of his analysis he emphasized the major themes invoked by modern Austrian economists when discussing negative externalities. In particular, he addressed the problem of conflicting property usage and the importance of clearly defining and enforcing property rights as a remedy.

It is clear from Menger's analysis that he was not thinking strictly of overt acts such as theft, but also of more subtle forms of conflicting property usage as would arise in modern discussions of externalities. Menger argued that private property is only necessary with economic goods, i.e., goods whose quantities are scarce relative to the desires of consumers. A truly non-economic good would not necessitate private ownership. According to Menger, this would include goods such as, in most cases, air for breathing and water for drinking. But he argues that in different circumstances a particular good's status may be on the borderline between economic and non-economic, and as Menger puts it, "misuse or ignorance on the part of some members of the economy [with respect to the utilization of the good] may easily become injurious to others . . . ." He further concludes that "for these and similar reasons the phenomenon of private property can also be observed in the case of goods that appear to us still, with respect to other aspects of economic life, as non-economic goods" (p. 105).

Although Menger does not give examples, the situations discussed above are clearly analogous to problems of air and water pollution. In the absence of pollution, clean air may be a non-economic or free good and therefore no property rights to the air need be enforced or even in place. Once the air is polluted, or misused as Menger put it, there may be "injurious" effects on others, i.e., a negative externality arises, transforming clean air into an economic good.

It is also clear that he saw the remedy to this type of problem in a property rights solution. In Menger's analysis, it is these types of negative externalities that explain why, as part of the natural evolution of societies, property rights to some otherwise non-economic goods may evolve. To reiterate, Menger's analysis was a positive attempt to explain the necessity for and eventual evolution of a property rights structure. But the normative conclusions that seem to automatically derive from Menger's arguments are similar to the modern Austrian analysis. In light of Menger's approach it is easy to understand why, for modern Austrians, an externality problem is a problem for property rights analysis not a problem for social cost/benefit analysis. (We will discuss below why, for Menger, like modern Austrians, it could not be the latter.) As Menger concludes, "property, therefore, like human economy, is not an arbitrary invention but rather the only practically possible solution of the problem" (p. 97).

Before looking at Menger's approach to the issue of external benefits it is important to examine his view of what in modern terms is called social cost/benefit analysis. The subjectivist approach of modern Austrians leads to a rejection of externalities analysis in terms of exact calculations of social costs and benefits. And since, in the standard Pigouvian framework, it is only comparisons of marginal social costs and benefits that gives rise to the conclusion that the presence of external benefits is evidence of market failure, there would be no reason why Austrians would come to similar conclusions. The origins of this modern Austrian position on the question of social welfare analysis, and consequently the social consequences of positive external effects, can clearly be found in Menger's writings.

In several passages Menger implies that he would have to reject any approach to externalities based strictly on cost-benefit analysis. When discussing the nature of value Menger states that "not only the nature but also the measure of value is subjective. Goods always have value to certain economizing individuals and this value is determined . . . only by these individuals" (p. 146). And in a different context Menger explicitly rejects the idea of using objective measures of individual wealth in any attempt to measure social welfare. He states that:

> The sum of economic goods at the disposal of individual economizing members of society for the purpose of satisfying their special individual needs obviously does not constitute wealth in the economic sense of the term . . . when inferences running from this [measure] to the welfare of the people or when phenomena resulting from contacts between the various economizing individuals, are involved . . . [this method] must necessarily lead to frequent errors. (p. 113, emphasis added)

In light of these statements, it would appear that Menger would reject the modern Pigouvian approach which analyzes the effects of externalities, both negative and positive, in terms of concrete measures of social welfare. If we compare Menger's position on this issue to that of Pigou we get some insight as to why the two economists spawned very different traditions, not only with respect to externalities analysis, but also with respect to welfare economics in general. In contrast to Menger, Pigou argues that economic welfare is objectively measurable. He states that "economic welfare . . . can be brought directly or indirectly into a relation with a money measure" (p. 31). Furthermore, Pigou argues that money is an appropriate measure of not only private but also social economic welfare. Arguing directly contrary to Menger, Pigou carries his analysis to its logical conclusion:

> . . . economic welfare and the national dividend are thus coordinate, in such wise as any description of the content of one of them implies a corresponding description of the content of the other. (Pigou, p. 31)

Given the contrast between the positions of Menger and Pigou on measuring economic welfare, it is only logical that modern economists in the Mengerian and Pigouvian traditions would take significantly different approaches to welfare economics and externalities analysis.

It can be shown that, at least in particular instances, Menger himself tended to view production and market processes that generate external benefits as socially beneficial, in that greater benefits are created than are intended by the actors directly participating in the process. The best example of this is Menger's evolutionary theory of the origin of money.

In his analysis, the fact that actions on the part of certain perceptive individuals generate positive externalities plays a crucial role in transforming a society from one based on barter to one based on monetary exchange. Menger argues that primitive societies naturally evolve through stages of exchange. The typical primitive economy will be transformed from a system based on pure barter, or direct exchange, to first a general recognition that more wants can be satisfied through indirect exchange to, ultimately, the widespread use of some medium of exchange, or money.

The movement from direct to indirect exchange takes place gradually. Relatively astute individuals realize that they can more fully satisfy their wants by exchanging what they have to trade for certain exceptionally marketable items, rather than attempting to trade for what they want to consume directly. These items allow the individuals to facilitate their own exchanges in their attempt to ultimately gain the commodities that are desired for direct consumption. As time passes, this practice becomes more and more widespread until one or a very few extremely marketable commodities become universally accepted in exchange, i.e., evolve into money. In other words certain commodities will be transformed from having only use value, to having both use value and exchange value, to having primarily exchange value.

This evolution takes place, in large part, because of certain positive externalities that are generated throughout the process which facilitates the transformation. Initially, a good's widespread salability for its use value is what gives it value to some individuals solely for exchange purposes. In other words, each additional individual who demands the product solely for its use value confers a benefit on those who have no direct use for the good by making it more marketable and therefore valuable to them in facilitating exchange. Market exchanges begin to occur that cause marginal private and "social" benefit to diverge. This divergence acts as a catalyst for furthering the process.

Once the good's exchange value is recognized by some individuals, the process of moving the good toward predominantly having exchange value begins to snowball, again because of positive external effects that are generated as part of the process. An externality which is explicitly recognized by Menger can be called the imitation effect. Once the concept of indirect exchange is recognized by some individuals, light is shed on the process for other individuals who observe the success of the initial transactions. As these people imitate the successful method of facilitating exchange and therefore satisfying their wants, others observe and imitate their successes, etc. As Menger stated it:

> Since there is no better way in which men can become enlightened about their economic interests than by observation of the economic success of those who employ the correct means of achieving their ends, it is evident that nothing favored the rise of money so much as the long practiced and economically profitable, acceptance of eminently saleable commodities in exchange for all others by the most discerning and most capable of economizing individuals. (p. 261)

An important point to make is that Menger describes this process, which has as a crucial element the existence of positive externalities, in order to prove that money arises as part of the spontaneous market order and that it "is not an invention of the state" (p. 261). Contrary to Menger's assessment, modern welfare economics argues that the existence of positive externalities is an explanation of why certain goods will not be produced in private markets and therefore why it is necessary for the state to subsidize, in part or in whole, their production. In Menger's theory of the origins of money it is obvious that if it weren't for the existence of positive external effects at each stage of the evolutionary process the good, money would not arise as a natural part of private economies. Ironically, in modern terminology, Menger seems to have been arguing that it is actually certain public goods aspects of money's evolution that insures that it will be produced in the absence of state intervention. This results from his viewing the generation of the external benefits as part of an ongoing, disequilibrium process rather than in terms of an otherwise fully equilibrated static state of affairs. Menger focuses on the chain of events that the external benefits give rise to, identifying the "unintended consequences" that result (see Butos, 1985).

**Eugen von Böhm-Bawerk**

Neither Böhm-Bawerk or Wieser addressed the issue of negative externalities or the problem of conflicting uses of property, but both provided some insights into the more contemporary Austrian view of positive externalities. Böhm-Bawerk was clearly the most explicit of the early Austrians in discussing this issue. His relevant work is an 1881 essay entitled "Whether Legal Rights and Relationships are Economic Goods" (1962), which builds on Menger's earlier discussion of the nature of goods. Böhm-Bawerk explicitly recognizes, as a positive observation, that the goods that are typically produced by the state are also goods that tend to generate positive externalities. It is worth quoting him at length on this issue.

> . . . only a tiny fraction of the total services derived from the state's institutions impresses itself upon any individual as a direct and positive rendition of service. The individuals comprising the community are the recipients of far greater advantages partly in the form of a far flung system of distribution; and partly in the negative form of protection from harmful disturbances.
>
> Persons for whom wrongs are righted by a judge in a court of law are not the only participants in the benefits of the state activities on behalf of right and justice which are performed by civil and criminal court judges. All others, including those who never see a court of law, share in these benefits too . . . because of the respect for law that prevails throughout the land by reason of the activities of those same judges. Every resident of any metropolitan center shares indirectly in the benefits emanating from the activities of the quarantine and sanitation or public health forces that operate at the national borders to prevent the introduction of epidemic diseases; he also shares in the benefits derived from the activities of all teachers and educators who, by giving intellectual and moral training to the entire body of our youth, train all persons to become his useful fellow citizens . . . (pp. 132-133)

What is particularly interesting for our purposes is that Böhm-Bawerk emphasizes all of this not in an attempt to place the goods provided by the state in a special category of goods that wouldn't be produced otherwise, but to show that they are not special. He argues that the state produces a collection of goods that are not unlike goods that are produced in private markets. He states that the person who benefits indirectly from these goods produced by the state also "benefits from the activities of all private . . . promoters of industry and from those . . . private individuals who contribute to the smooth functioning of traffic and trade . . ." (p. 133). In fact he goes even further (unwittingly) toward desanctifying the "public" nature of state produced goods by concluding that the indirect beneficiaries of these goods also "share[] in the benefits arising from the activity of all the individuals in the community who make any direct or indirect contribution to the general welfare" (p. 133).

The direct implication here is that goods and services that generate external benefits are not a special category of goods that cause peculiar problems for a market economy. Böhm-Bawerk points out that these types of goods are produced side by side by both private and public concerns, and in both cases the external benefits themselves are discussed with only positive connotations.

It is true that Böhm-Bawerk did not directly discuss the possibility that a good might be purely public and therefore not be produced at all in private markets. In other words, he did not discuss a situation where the external benefits associated with a good would be so great that they would create insurmountable free rider problems for private producers. There are indications, though, that he would have viewed this problem as simply one of the infinite number of reasons why a good might not end up being produced in certain markets. Thus the modern Austrian view of this aspect of the positive externality issue also may have roots in Böhm-Bawerk's writings. Böhm-Bawerk argues, in a general discussion about the nature of goods, that whether or not something will be produced depends on the existence of what he calls "positive" and "negative" factors. Unless these positive and negative factors come together in an advantageous way, the good will not be produced. This concept is best understood through Böhm-Bawerk's own words.

> Every economic advantage, if it is to eventuate, requires, on the one hand, a positive causative element that will effect the advantage, but it also requires, on the other hand, a host of negative presuppositions, presuppositions that there will be an absence of elements which would prevent or vitiate the positively useful progress of events . . . . (p. 130)

Although not specified, it would seem that one of the negative presuppositions that would be necessary for the production of any good is that there is the absence of an insurmountable free rider problem. Furthermore, it is implied that Böhm-Bawerk would not have considered such a "negative presupposition" as something that merits special consideration by economists. He concludes that

> it [is] impermissible for us to make any special computation for some selected individual instance out of the entire class of negative factors simply because for some special reason our attention is specially and conspicuously directed to that single factor. (p. 130)

**Friedrich von Wieser**

In regards to externalities, Friedrich von Wieser is as notable for the arguments that he didn't make as for the those he did. First, it is important to note that Wieser, along with early Austrian economist Emil Sax, has been included as a precursor of modern public finance economics [Musgrave and Peacock (1958), and Weber (1973)]. This is especially notable because this branch of neoclassical economics is based more than any other on Pigouvian externalities analysis. In his *Social Economics* (1967: first edition 1914, second edition 1924, English translation 1927.), Wieser discussed at length his view of the role of the state and the principles of taxation. What is interesting for our purposes is that his discussion did not center on the issue of externalities or the public nature of any goods. For Wieser, what defined the state was not the type of goods that it produced but the way it raised and distributed its revenues. Hence, he did not speak of public or collective goods but of, what he called, collective expenditures. In fact, he openly rejected the idea that the distinction between the public and private economies is to be made in terms of the type of good each sector produces. In response to what he saw as the prevalent view of his time, Wieser writes:

> Modern theories look upon activities of the state as a special sort of production, an immaterial kind ... [producing] the intangible products of peace and legal security.
>
> Such views only serve to obscure the nature of the public economy. Essentially it is not to be distinguished in concept from the private economy ... both serve the purposes of turning to the greatest possible usefulness the commodities that are found in the economic quantitative relation. (p. 420)

From this Wieser goes on to describe, in his view, what truly distinguishes the public economy.

> But the state in its economy has unique means of power placed at its disposal . . . [P]ublic economic income [is] . . . entirely unknown to private economy and [is] no way related to exchange or production . . . the principles observed in levying taxes have nothing in common with the law of price. (p. 420)

As mentioned above, his discussion of the public economy proceeds in terms of collective expenditure not in terms of collective goods. In the midst of defining "collective expenditures" Wieser is especially sensitive to the possibility that the word "collective" might be misapplied and specifically points out that it refers to means (the form of payment) and not ends (the particular goods purchased). He states that:

> Collective expenditures are collective in that they employ common means under unified direction . . . They are not so much collective in the sense that they serve collective needs . . . In the main the economy of the state caters to the same [needs] . . . to which private economies cater. (p. 422)

The point to be made here is that, although Wieser advocated an extensive role for the state in the provision of economic goods and is often cited in neoclassical public finance literature, there is no evidence that his advocacy is derived from a concern with external benefits and public goods. In fact, his entire discussion of the "Theory of the State Economy" (pp. 419-436) lacks any indication that he felt goods which generate external benefits warrant any special attention by what he called the "public economy."

### Concluding Remarks on Menger, Böhm-Bawerk, and Wieser

Although Menger's view of goods, or economic processes, that generate external benefits can only be inferred and Böhm-Bawerk and Wieser did not discuss issues related to negative externalities or the conflicting use of property, there is a unifying theme in the analysis of all three of the Austrian school's founders. That unifying theme is, arguably, also the most distinctive feature of the approach to externalities taken by most modern Austrians. Concisely stated, it is that goods which generate external benefits are not goods that, per se, create any special problem for a market economy. In both Böhm-Bawerk and Wieser, it is explicitly stated that this is not the defining characteristic of goods that the state does or should produce. With Menger's theory of the origins of money, it is at least implied that, rather than being a hindrance to market processes, the generation of external benefits may in some cases help to facilitate these processes and result in more widespread social benefits.[4]

This theme can be taken together with Menger's view of the relationship between what we now call negative externalities and private property. When this is done, the more modern assessments of externalities found in the works of Mises and Rothbard can be viewed as an extension of at least an attitude toward the issue that has existed throughout the school's history.

## CONCLUSION

In this chapter we have examined the analysis of externalities as it has developed in the Austrian school. In doing so, some significant differences between the neoclassical and Austrian analysis have been revealed, particularly when assessing the normative consequences of external effects.

Contrary to the standard Pigouvian approach, which argues that both positive and negative externalities will have adverse consequences for economic welfare, Austrian economists, following the lead of Mises, and later, Rothbard, have dissented from this view. In general they have argued that only those externalities which are the result of ambiguously defined or unenforced property rights can be judged as having negative effects on the efficiency of a market process. Such externality problems are usually associated with negative external effects, leading most Austrians to concentrate their analysis on issues such as air and water pollution. On the other hand, since most positive external effects that are generated do not involve property-rights conflicts, external benefits are generally judged to be welfare enhancing. If an external benefit "problem" arises that is the result of ambiguously defined entitlements, then some form of public policy which focuses on establishing those rights may be advocated. The sole example of this in the literature is Mises' discussion patent and copyright laws.

The neoclassical approach to externalities theory, and in particular the symmetrical conclusions regarding the welfare effects of positive and negative externalities, are implied by the normative standards described by a perfectly competitive general equilibrium. Thus far we have made no attempt to identify a similar standard of economic welfare that would give rise to the approach advocated by most Austrian economists. We have instead, simply pointed out that the Austrian school has rejected the perfectly competitive welfare standard and has emphasized a market process analysis that is based on a strict interpretation of subjective value theory. This can explain why the Austrian literature contains an approach that is different from the standard analysis, but it cannot explain how the particulars of that approach have been derived.

The following chapter takes up the issue of economic welfare analysis as it has developed in the writings of Austrian economists. No normative economic assessment can be complete without a grounding in a theory of welfare economics or efficiency. To date, few attempts have been made to derive normative conclusions about externalities from any of the alternative notions of efficiency that have been developed by Austrian economists (see Cordato 1980 & 1989). In other words, welfare economics and externalities analysis, to the extent they have developed at all, have been pursued independently of each other. The primary purpose of the chapter that follows is to complete the "stock taking" with respect to the current state of Austrian externalities theory by bringing these two elements together. As part of this exercise, the welfare economics of Murray Rothbard and Israel Kirzner are critically assessed for both internal coherency and relevancy for the evaluation of external effects.

## NOTES

1 This issue is discussed at greater length in chapter 4.

2 In using the terms positive and negative externalities here, the conventional distinctions are made. An act taken by individual A is defined as generating a positive or negative externality depending upon how it enters into B's utility function. From a definitional standpoint there is an inherent symmetry between positive and negative externalities, just as there is an inherent symmetry between all costs and benefits. To eliminate an external cost, by definition, is to convey a benefit. This can be viewed in terms of the standard definition where A's activity is a positive or negative entry into (a passive) B's utility function (see "Introduction," note 1). If A discontinues an activity that is having a negative impact on B's utility, there will be a positive effect on B's overall level of satisfaction. This is why pollution control laws are sometimes considered a "public good," even though pollution is typically considered a negative externality, while public goods are typically associated with external benefits. When Austrians, such as Mises and Rothbard, allude to an asymmetry between positive and negative externalities they are referring strictly to the normative consequences of external effects and are not denying this definitional symmetry.

3 Unless otherwise stated all references in this section are from Hayek, 1979. Other similar but less extensive discussions of externalities can be found in Hayek, 1948 (pp. 107-118), 1960 (pp. 340-356), and 1985 (pp. 144-145).

4 It should be noted that all three authors clearly believed that the state should provide certain goods and services that are now referred to as public goods. The point to be made is that there is no attempt on their part to justify the provision of these goods on the basis of external effects that their provision generates. This is in contrast to their contemporary, the early Austrian economist Emil Sax, who did argue explicitly that the nature of the state is to provide for "collective needs . . . where no specific benefit share can be determined for the individual" (Neck, p. 10). Sax also distinguishes between "universal" and "particular" collective activities of the state and it has been argued that the former could be characterized in terms of the "external and spillover effects" that they generate (Neck, p. 20). Given that Sax was a contemporary of Böhm-Bawerk and Weiser (in Austria), it suggests that their neglect of collective goods arguments for the state was not an oversight.

# 2

# EXTERNALITIES AND MODERN AUSTRIAN THEORIES OF ECONOMIC WELFARE: PROBLEMS AND PROMISES

> In Austria, economics has never had direct political aims in spite of the close connection of the Austrian marginal utility theory with utilitarian philosophy. The Austrians were preoccupied with value theory and never elaborated a detailed theory of welfare economics. (Myrdal, 1955)

Although modern Austrians have moved away from the preoccupation with value theory attributed by Myrdal to the early Austrians, little attention has been devoted to developing an Austrian theory of welfare economics. In the case of externalities, the Austrian approach discussed in Chapter 1 is not explicitly based on any clearly defined efficiency or welfare criteria.

Once it is realized that most Austrians have not accepted the Pigouvian welfare standard, the Austrian approach to positive externalities becomes partially intelligible, at least in a negative sense. Specifically, in the absence of Pigouvian marginal analysis there is no reason to interpret external benefits differently, for normative purposes, than any other type of benefit. But the relationship between the normative effects of externalities and property rights, as is primarily emphasized in the Austrian analysis of negative externalities, is not quite so easily interpreted. With no clearly defined normative benchmark the conclusion--that only externalities involving a conflict in property usage have policy implications--cannot be completely understood or justified.

Since the criticism of orthodox externalities theory presented here centers around fundamental disagreements with neoclassical welfare economics, it is incumbent upon Austrians to present a coherent alternative. Indeed, no credible assessment of externalities from an economics perspective can be made without such an alternative.

The purpose of this chapter is to critically assess the current state of Austrian efficiency theory and welfare economics. There are two normative standards that have been explicitly proposed, if not completely developed. It is important to assess the strengths and weaknesses of these approaches in order to lay the groundwork for further refinements and the establishment of a sound normative foundation for externalities analysis. Furthermore, in order to round out the discussion from the previous chapter we will investigate here the extent to which these different standards can be used as a justification for the Austrian approach to externalities as it has developed.

In the literature of modern Austrian economics there are primarily two distinct, although related, economic welfare standards that have been suggested as a backdrop for policy. Each of these, when used as a standard for normative analysis, would give rise to the approach to externalities discussed in chapter 1. One of these standards was introduced by and is primarily associated with Rothbard while the second has been most extensively detailed by Israel Kirzner. Although neither of these approaches have been developed to the extent that neoclassical welfare economics has, one of the two, that discussed by Kirzner, has been developed much more extensively. Consequently, this approach or some variation of it, has been widely adopted among Austrians involved in normative analysis (Armentano, 1990, pp. 29-30; Rizzo and O'Driscoll, 1985, pp. 113-119; O'Driscoll 1977; Lavoie, 1985, pp. 34-39; Cordato, 1989). In addition, it can be viewed as an ex post efficiency rationalization for much of Hayek's analysis. [1967 (1935); 1948 (1935A, 1945A)]

## ROTHBARD'S CRITERIA OF DEMONSTRATED PREFERENCE

Rothbard formulates his normative economic benchmark in terms of maximizing social utility. Consistent with general Austrian methodology, he attempts to tie his welfare standard directly to individual valuation. In doing this he adopts an approach to deducing preferences that is found in Mises and is similar to, although not the same as, Samuelson's "revealed preference" (see Rothbard, 1977, pp. 5-7).[1] Mises argues that an individual will always act in a way that is consistent with his value scale (1966, p. 95). In other words, in all courses of action a person will always adopt his subjectively determined highest valued alternative. According to Mises:

> . . . the scale of values or wants manifests itself only in the reality of action. These scales have no independent existence apart from the actual behavior of individuals . . . Every action is always in perfect agreement with the scale of values or wants . . . (Mises, 1966, p. 95)

From this starting point both Mises, Rothbard, and most other Austrian economists, argue that a person's highest valued alternative can be deduced from the actions that are taken. In other words people reveal their preferences through action.

This concept, which Rothbard calls "demonstrated preference," serves as the foundation for his economic welfare analysis. He argues that voluntary action will always, ex ante, be viewed as welfare enhancing from the point of view of the individual taking the action. Rothbard then concludes that "if we define an increase in social utility in the Paretian manner" (1976, p. 98) evaluations and proclamations about social welfare can be made without the use of interpersonal utility comparisons. But Rothbard adopts a strict individualist, non-equilibrium interpretation of the standard Paretian rule. It allows for no social welfare functions and is not dependent on the attainment of any equilibrium or Pareto optimal state. In Rothbard's view, an economist can claim that there has been an increase in social utility only when "one or more persons gain in utility while nobody loses" (1976, p. 98). By coupling this rule with "demonstrated preference," he reasons that all free market activity is welfare enhancing. Rothbard states that:

> [a free market exchange] is voluntarily undertaken by both parties. Therefore, the very fact that an exchange takes place demonstrates that both parties benefit **(or more strictly, expect to benefit)** from the exchange. The fact that both parties choose the exchange demonstrates that they both benefit. The free market is the name for all the voluntary exchanges that take place in the world. Since every exchange demonstrates unanimity of benefit for both parties concerned, we must conclude that the free market benefits all its participants. In other words, welfare economics can make the statement that the free market increases social utility . . . (Rothbard, 1977, p. 27, emphasis added).

It should be pointed out that Rothbard's conclusions concerning welfare and social utility can be taken to task on several crucial points. The validity of his approach will be discussed below. First, though, it is interesting to draw out the implications of his normative criteria for the analysis of external effects. One problem that arises in doing this stems from the fact that Rothbard does not, in the context of his welfare economics, define what is meant by a voluntary act. This must be done before it can be determined whether or not an exchange is voluntary and therefore welfare enhancing. It is clear from Rothbard's other writings that he would consider an act to be voluntary to the extent that it involves the use of one's own property in a way that he sees fit.[2] In other words, a determination of whether or not an act is voluntary would center around the use of private property. A coercive act, which according to Rothbard always makes at least one person worse off and therefore reduces social welfare, would be one that violates the private property rights of a market participant. He declares that:

> The normative principle I am suggesting . . . is simply this: No action should be considered illicit or illegal unless it invades, agresses against, the person or just property of another. (Rothbard, 1982A, p. 60)

With this approach to voluntary action in mind, Rothbard's welfare criteria can be applied to externalities in a straight forward manner. Any use of one's property by another without the former's permission would be considered a coerced exchange. It would violate the Paretian rule and therefore reduce social welfare. This gives rise to Rothbard's and Mises' normative conclusion regarding negative externalities. A pollution externality is a social problem because the pollution interferes with the use of property by its "legitimate" owner, i.e., it represents a coerced exchange (Rothbard, 1982A). In generating the pollution the polluter is being made better off at the expense of the recipient of the externality.

External benefits, to the extent that they are actually generated, as in the case of a type 1 externality, would have to be considered welfare enhancing from Rothbard's perspective. It involves no violation of property rights and makes one or more persons better off without making anyone worse off. The generation of positive externalities represents a Pareto superior move. The fact that the result may be inconsistent with a hypothetically derived state of Pareto optimality for that moment in time would be irrelevant in Rothbard's disequilibrium framework. He makes no reference to a "welfare maximized" state of the world when developing his Paretian criteria.

Neither would the results associated with a type 2 externality have negative connotations from the perspective of demonstrated preference. The fact that the good in question does not get produced results from a demonstrated preference not to make certain exchanges. From Rothbard's perspective, the reason's behind that action, or in this case inaction, would be beyond the scope of economic analysis. In other words, the fact that the exchange is not being made because one of the parties is attempting to obtain the good for free or because transactions costs are too high, will have no role in any normative analysis made from the perspective of demonstrated preference. From Rothbard's point of view it must be concluded that, given Mises' type 2 externalities result, at the very least, social welfare has not been reduced.

While Rothbard never examines externalities in light of his theory of welfare economics, it could easily serve as a normative backdrop for the conclusions that were reached by Mises and most subsequent Austrian economists. With external benefits, the argument that exchanges are not made because of "excessive" transaction costs is irrelevant. As has traditionally been the case in Austrian economics, there is no basis for a normative distinction between transaction costs and other costs. The preferences being demonstrated are consistent will all perceived costs and benefits.

The most common criticism of demonstrated preference as a welfare guide is that Rothbard does not allow for any consideration of harm that is not demonstrated, i.e., psychic harm. The welfare effects of envy, trauma, etc. are ruled out of his model. The voluntary activities of some people may have negative psychic effects on others, causing a decline in their level of satisfaction. To the extent that this occurs, some people will be made better off at the expense of others and there will not be an unambiguous increase in "social utility."

Once this criticism is recognized other problems become readily apparent. One implication is that interpersonal utility comparisons cannot, as Rothbard claims, be avoided. In order to conclude that a market exchange unambiguously increases "social utility," the effects on everyone's satisfaction must be considered and compared; even those whose preferences are not being demonstrated. Rothbard's approach does not eliminate this problem, but simply ignores it. Oddly enough, in a different context, Rothbard admits this point. He argues that given a free market exchange by two parties, A and B, "there might be one or more people in existence who dislike and envy A or B, and who therefore experience pain and psychic loss because the object of their envy has improved his lot. We cannot conclude from the mere fact of exchange that 'everyone' is better off, and we can therefore not leap to the valuational idea of social utility" (1973B, p. 36). While this statement implies a recantation of his earlier welfare theory, Rothbard has not acknowledged the contradiction.

But there are even more damaging criticisms to be made of Rothbard's approach. By focussing strictly on demonstrated preferences and ex ante evaluations, he rules out all consideration of costs and therefore the possibility of utility loss. Cost is the foregone satisfaction associated with activities that are not undertaken. By definition costs cannot be demonstrated. Therefore, in Rothbard's model only benefits, that is, utility gains, are recognized. The narrow focus on ex ante action restricts the analysis to a consideration of expectations about the rewards from activities that are being pursued. By definition, though, people always expect to benefit, relative to the alternatives, from every action that is undertaken. This is true under any institutional arrangement. An action taken at the point of a gun is expected to result in an increase in utility relative to the available alternatives.

It can only be determined ex post whether or not the desired goal was reached and an increase or loss in utility was experienced. Clearly, even in a free market, if an individual expends a large amount of resources in pursuit of a goal and then finds out that the services or satisfaction that he anticipated receiving were not forthcoming, his efforts would have been in vain. Clearly he would have experienced a loss in utility.

The point is that the economist must wait for the ex post results of action in order to determine whether utility has been increased or decreased. Rothbard's conclusions would only hold in an error free world of perfect knowledge, where expectations necessarily coincide with results. It is not surprising, then, that Rothbard comes to the conclusion that all free market activities imply increases in social utility. He rules out any possibility of utility loss in constructing his model.

Another fundamental problem with Rothbard's welfare economics is that it ignores the fact that preferences are expressed sequentially through time, as part of a general set of goal oriented activities. The actor in Rothbard's framework is operating in a static world where actions are undertaken in isolation from one another. The fact that all preferences are "demonstrated" within the context of a means-ends framework is missed. This emphasis on static, unconnected action has led to conclusions with regard to both individual and social welfare that are obviously incorrect.

For example, one analyst, in a strict application of Rothbard's social utility theory, argues that, given two individuals pursuing an employment opportunity, the individual whose offer is rejected suffers no loss in utility (Osterfeld). In Rothbard's framework, the person whose salary request was rejected is no worse off for the failed attempt. "He did not have the job before he made the offer; he does not have the job after his offer was rejected. Thus his . . . real world utility plane is unchanged" (Osterfeld, p. 81). But, consistent with Rothbard's theory, this analysis ignores the fact that the rejection was the culmination of an attempt to obtain a particular goal, i.e., the job. The attainment of goals are associated with utility gains while the employment of means are associated with opportunity costs or disutility. If certain means are employed in order to attain an end that is never achieved then opportunities are forgone without a resulting payoff, and the actor will have suffered a net reduction in utility. Given the typical costs associated with a job search--preparing a resume, going to an employment agency, filling out an application--the individual in the example above would have to have suffered a net loss in utility. This obvious conclusion is avoided by separating out particular actions of individuals from their overall means-ends framework.

These criticisms have implications that relate directly to externalities analysis. If only external effects that are demonstrated can be evaluated by Rothbard's normative criteria, a strict interpretation of his approach would have to conclude that any harms or benefits that are not demonstrated do not actually exist. For instance, an example of a negative externality that does not involve a violation of property rights was discussed in chapter 1. In this example, individual A imposed psychic harm on his neighbor, individual B, by storing junk cars on his front lawn. As was pointed out, the standard Austrian conclusion with respect to this type of situation is that a non-voluntary remedy to this problem could not unambiguously improve social welfare. But if Rothbard's welfare criteria was guiding the analysis the fact that an externality was even being generated would have to be denied.

In light of these criticisms, Rothbard's welfare economics does not offer much promise as a general guide for externalities theory or policy. His approach begs many of the questions that would have to be answered if an analysis of externalities were to be considered complete. The problems noted above could also explain why Rothbard's normative standard has not been widely adopted by other Austrian economists in discussions of appropriate approaches to welfare economics. While Rothbard, along with Mises, has established the standard assessment of externalities from an Austrian perspective, we must look elsewhere for a coherent welfare economics to serve as a backdrop for that assessment.

## KIRZNER: EFFICIENCY AS PLAN COORDINATION

To the extent that Austrian economists have discussed issues in terms of efficiency, it has been the concept of plan coordination, as made explicit and elaborated by Kirzner, that has been commonly used. Most often it has been invoked as a backdrop for defining and discussing the normative implications of competition and monopoly (Armentano, 1990; Kirzner, 1973). It has also been argued that monetary theory and policy is best seen in light of this type of efficiency standard (Garrison, 1978, p. 169). Kirzner's theory is clearly the most well developed and thought out conception of welfare economics in modern Austrian economics.

### Individual Efficiency and Social Efficiency

Kirzner's approach is distinguished by the fact that it is primarily developed in a disequilibrium or market process setting. But it does not completely avoid equilibrium theorizing and the notion of general equilibrium does play a role. In defining perfect efficiency, he describes an equilibrium world where there is complete plan coordination. At any given point in time, with preference scales held constant, an ideal market process will move towards this state. But unlike Pigouvian welfare analysis, Kirzner sees the particular end-state pattern of resource allocation as hypothetical and irrelevant for real world appraisals of social efficiency (1963, p. 298). Instead of dwelling on the perfectly efficient equilibrium, Kirzner focuses on the relative efficiency of any given disequilibrium market process that might be taking place. He describes the purpose of his analysis this way:

> . . . it is the market process that is being judged rather than the state of equilibrium the process leads toward . . . After all, in a changing world, a state of market equilibrium, as we have seen is hardly an attainable goal. The precise degree in which the state of market equilibrium deviates from the conditions of optimality is therefore . . . a distinctly academic question. (Kirzner, 1963, p. 299)

A second distinction of this efficiency standard is that, consistent with methodological individualism and like Rothbard's theory, individual and social efficiency are seen as mutually consistent. If particular actions are efficient from the perspective of the individuals making up society they will also be considered socially efficient. This can be compared to standard Pigouvian analysis where actions deemed to be efficient from the perspective of individual market participants may lead to distinctly inefficient outcomes when viewed from "society's perspective." This is seen most clearly in the case of positive externalities. An activity generating positive externalities that are not either internalized or compensated for is judged to be socially inefficient, even though all of the relevant market participants are, from their own perspective, acting rationally and experiencing positive gains in utility. This kind of clash between individual and social welfare is not only inconsistent with Kirzner's, and Rothbard's, welfare economics, but could not be sustained by any theory of social efficiency developed from a strictly Austrian perspective.

Kirzner begins his analysis by focusing on the determinants of efficient activity from the perspective of the individual's means-ends framework. (A more elaborate discussion of individual efficiency will be pursued in the following chapter.) Since all action is seen as purposeful, i.e., goal seeking, efficiency for an individual is viewed in terms of the extent to which his activities, the means employed, are consistent with the goals or ends that are hoped to be accomplished (1963, pp. 33-34). This will depend upon the extent to which the individual has knowledge of the means available and the extent to which they are suitable for achieving the desired goal or program of goals. The efficiency of the individual's activities will improve as he obtains more knowledge that is relevant to those activities.

It is important to note that the individual in Kirzner's model is not presented in terms of the utility maximizing framework of neoclassical economics, where individual efficiency is achieved by equalizing given marginal rates of substitution. Kirzner postulates an individual that is making decisions through time. This individual is more akin to Buchanan's "artifactual man" (1979A), where some future state of affairs (the goal) is imagined and, under conditions of uncertainty, attempts are made to achieve it. According to Kirzner:

> . . . in making plans, individuals have in mind given sets of goals. With respect to this set of goals, they seek a consistent, efficient course of action. (Kirzner, 1963, p. 34)

In Kirzner's framework social efficiency is derived directly from individual efficiency. Once individuals find it advantageous to pursue their goals in a cooperative setting, through exchange and the division of labor, the concern is with the basis upon which the cooperative setting, i.e., the economic process, can be judged efficient. Kirzner suggests the following criteria:

> . . . the efficiency of the social system . . . depends on the degree of coordination with which the separate activities of the participants are carried on. (Kirzner, 1963, p. 36)

By coordination Kirzner is referring to the mutual compatibility of plans among market participants (1963, p. 36). Therefore an economic process is judged efficient to the extent that it harmonizes the plans of individuals in the pursuit of their goals. As with efficiency for the individual, social efficiency depends on knowledge. In this case, it is the knowledge held by market participants of relative scarcities and the desires of their fellow market participants (1963, pp. 301-302). To the extent that this type of knowledge exists, people will be able to exploit a greater number of opportunities for mutually beneficial exchange. Given that exchange of this nature implies the coordination of plans on the part of the traders, Kirzner reasons that an economic system can be judged efficient to the extent that it generates knowledge of mutually beneficial exchange possibilities.

For Kirzner, improvements in knowledge are synonymous with increased plan coordination among market participants. As the market process brings new information to light, the plans of market participants become more closely coordinated and social efficiency is improved. He argues that,

> . . . the movement from disequilibrium to equilibrium is at once a movement from imperfect knowledge to perfect knowledge and from uncoordination to coordination . . . [the] learning process . . . nudges individual plans into closer and closer coordination. (Kirzner, 1973, pp. 218-219)

## Knowledge, Coordination, and Equilibrium

As noted above, a state of perfect efficiency is associated with a world of complete coordination of plans, which, in turn, is synonymous with general equilibrium and a world of perfect knowledge. Kirzner makes the connection as follows:

> The state of equilibrium is the state in which all actions are perfectly coordinated, each market participant dovetailing his decisions with those which he (with complete accuracy) anticipates other participants will make. The perfection of knowledge which defines the state of equilibrium ensures complete coordination of individual plans. (Kirzner, 1973, p. 218).

In Kirzner's framework, knowledge, coordination, equilibration, and efficiency always move in the same direction. Improvements in knowledge will always be equilibrating and lead to increased plan coordination. By definition, this implies an improvement in social efficiency. Furthermore, with preferences held constant, the market process will generate improvements in information and coordination until a perfect knowledge, perfectly coordinated, and therefore, perfectly efficient end state is reached.

The role of the entrepreneur in this process is crucial. The social function of the entrepreneur is to facilitate plan coordination by exploiting profit opportunities. Price discrepancies, i.e., the existence of two prices in the same market for the same good, indicate a lack of plan coordination. Because of a lack of information concerning alternative trading partners, some consumers are paying higher prices and buying smaller quantities of the good than is necessary while presumably some marginal consumers are going without the good completely. Discoordination exists, then, between certain potential buyers and sellers. In exploiting the profit opportunities that arise from this incomplete knowledge the alert entrepreneur brings new and improved exchange opportunities to market participants. The result, according to Kirzner's theory, is always an increase in plan coordination and therefore an increase in social efficiency. Because of this, all successful entrepreneurial activity, where profit opportunities are accurately perceived and exploited, is seen as "equilibrating," i.e., as a movement in the direction of general equilibrium and "perfect efficiency." As Kirzner concludes:

> Each entrepreneurial discovery represents alertness to a hitherto unperceived interpersonal opportunity--an opportunity that depends on the coordinated plans of two separate individuals. As this "general" equilibrating process proceeds by competitive-entrepreneurial alertness, it identifies more and more uncoordinated situations, at the same time spreading the information perceived by entrepreneurial alertness among wider and wider circles in the market. (Kirzner, 1973, p. 222)

The use of general equilibrium in Kirzner's approach can be contrasted to the standard analysis of social efficiency. As already noted, Kirzner does not consider general equilibrium as an attainable goal and would never use as a starting point, particularly in normative discussions of efficiency, the assumption of general equilibrium prices or outputs. While invoking general equilibrium as a mental construct in order to delineate a world of perfect efficiency and to draw out the logical conclusion of a market process, Kirzner considers the efficiency problem itself under a "state of the world" that is always in disequilibrium. This is distinctly different from orthodox analysis of allocative efficiency, where a level of knowledge is given to the individual or society, and most of the time that level of knowledge is considered to be perfect. The knowledge problem, and therefore the coordination problem, is already solved in the standard efficiency framework. The assumption that all relevant means and ends are known in the Pigouvian model eliminates the coordination problem. The efficiency problem then becomes one of determining the precise pattern, or set of precise patterns, of resource usage that will maximize social welfare.

## Plan Coordination and Externalities[3]

An internal consistency can be recognized between the normative analysis of externalities typically associated with the Austrian school and Austrian welfare economics as presented by Kirzner. For Kirzner, if an activity leads to an improvement in knowledge and, hence, coordinates previously uncoordinated plans, that activity can be deemed efficient. Contrariwise, if an activity leads to the disruption and discoordination of plans then that activity would have to be considered inefficient.

Different kinds of externalities can be assessed with Kirzner's criteria in mind. Only those externalities that lead to a disruption of plans and/or the discoordination of plans among market participants should be considered inefficient. In a general sense, the traditional Austrian perspective on externalities follows from Kirzner's standard. But there are some areas of vagueness that suggest underlying problems with the use of plan coordination as a general standard for efficiency and social welfare.

The assessment of external benefits, from this perspective is quite clear. Positive externalities, per se, will have no adverse consequences. In other words, there is nothing discoordinating with respect to market participants' plans.

We can examine Mises' two types of positive externalities, discussed in chapter 1, in light of Kirzner's theory. To recall, a type 1 external benefit in Mises' framework is one that does not prevent the production of the good in question: it is analogous to a situation where the good is less than purely public. In the Kirznerian framework the equilibrium benchmark against which the actual market outcome is typically judged is considered unattainable. Furthermore, the actual equilibrium price and level of output is considered to be unspecifiable. Any equilibrium state in Kirzner's analysis, must be the result of the market process that has led up to it. Therefore, it cannot be argued that less than the efficient quantity is being produced. In fact, from Kirzner's perspective, this type of externality can only be considered efficiency enhancing. The production of this type of good not only furthers the goals of the producer and those who are participating directly in the market for this product but also furthers the interests of third parties who are not participating in the market. In this framework, Mises' type 1 externality can correctly be viewed as an unintended fringe benefit of the market process--one that is both coordinating and efficiency enhancing.

Mises' second type of externality is analogous to a pure public good where no one is willing to bear the costs of production, resulting in the good not being produced. For the reasons just discussed, there is no framework from which to argue that too little of the good is being produced. In other words, Kirzner's standard does not suggest that a production level of zero is any less optimal than any positive level of production.

At first glance it may appear that the potential presence of positive externalities, in this case, may be discoordinating given that certain opportunities for beneficial exchange are kept from materializing. In other words, because of potential positive external effects, transactions costs were increased, and what otherwise would have been an opportunity for mutually beneficial exchange did not come to fruition. But there is nothing in Kirzner's analysis that suggests transaction costs should be treated differently, for normative purposes, from other types of costs, i.e., transportation costs or labor costs. If an opportunity for exchange doesn't exist because transactions costs are too high then, given all the costs and benefits of making the exchange, it must be concluded that there simply is no opportunity for mutually beneficial exchange.

In Kirzner's framework, truly missed opportunities for exchange will always exist and will be discoordinating, but the standard case of public goods is not an example. A truly missed opportunity for exchange will exist only in the presence of what Kirzner calls "utter ignorance," i.e., when there is a complete lack of knowledge of the opportunity (1986).[4] From this criterion Mises' type 2 externality result does not represent a situation of discoordinated plans and therefore would not be considered inefficient. In other words, potential exchanges are forgone not because market participants are ignorant of the possibility of ex change but because the costs of making the exchange outweighed the expected benefits.

When applied to negative externalities, the implications of Kirzner's efficiency standard are less certain. There is no question that Kirzner's standard implies Mises' and Rothbard's normative assessment that externalities involving the conflicting use of property will give rise to market inefficiency. For example, if pollutants from a factory end up on property that is owned by someone other than the factory owner, and assuming that the externality disrupts the execution of at least some plans that person might have with respect to the use of his property, the existence of the externality must be deemed inefficient. If the externality involves the conflicting use of property where rights are not clearly defined, such as "publicly" owned waterways, forests, etc., then the lack of clearly defined rights will give rise to interpersonal conflicts and discoordination. This is consistent with what Kirzner sees as the "ideal" institutional setting for the operation of a market system (to be discussed at length in Chapters 3 and 4). He argues essentially that in order for a market system to flourish, property rights need to be clearly defined and strictly enforced (1963, p. 13).

A vagueness in applying Kirzner's efficiency standard to the issue of externalities arises with regard to certain kinds of negative third-party effects that do not involve conflicts in the use of property. That vagueness, I would argue, stems from a weakness in the coordination standard itself. This weakness involves discoordinating activities that, as Jack High has argued (1986), are an inherent part of the market process.[5] For example, in the competitive process it is often the case that the activities of one entrepreneur will disrupt plans that have been made by his competitors. If entrepreneur A discovers a less costly way to produce and sell a widget, he may disrupt the plans of his competitor, entrepreneur B, who has missed this opportunity to sell his widgets at a lower price. This activity would be coordinating with respect to the plans of A and the consumers of widgets, but discoordinating with respect to plans made by B.

This type of discoordination is explained within Kirzner's framework of analysis, but the explanation itself implies that the coordination standard cannot be strictly applied in every circumstance. As was discussed above, Kirzner's view of efficiency starts with the individual and the extent to which his means are consistent with the attainment of the sought after goal or set of goals. In the example above the discoordination was caused by the fact that B's original means were inconsistent with his ends. B's goal was to produce widgets in such a way that he could sell them for a profit. As the market process unfolded it became clear that his chosen course of action was based on erroneous expectations. Viewed from this perspective, the discoordination and therefore inefficiency was inherent in B's original means ends framework. B's failure was due to the fact that he did not accurately perceive the new conditions brought about by the activities of entrepreneur A. As the market process unfolded this misperception was revealed to B.

For Kirzner, this type of plan discoordination is inherent in a disequilibrium market process and is the result of errors in assessing markets, i.e., imperfect knowledge. He argues that, because of the incentives that are created by the system of profits and losses, even this type of plan discoordination will tend to be minimized in a competitive process. Entrepreneur B will be encouraged to revise his plans as his errors are exposed and losses are incurred (Kirzner, 1963, p. 304 and 1973 pp. 212-242). In other words, there would be no reason to make this type of plan discoordination the object of public policy.

This explanation, although consistent with Kirzner's framework of analysis, does not negate High's criticism. The fact remains that the activities of entrepreneur A had third-party effects that were discoordinating, i.e., that disrupted what otherwise would have been the coordinated plans of B with respect to his customers. Clearly, this kind of discoordinating activity is generally considered beneficial.

The Kirznerian explanation of this phenomenon itself suggests that the emphasis on coordination as an appropriate welfare standard may be misplaced. The elimination of error may be a more appropriate focus for our attention. While Kirzner has argued that the two are completely consistent, High's arguments imply that this is not the case.

## Coordination vs. Improvements in Knowledge

From Kirzner's perspective, in a perfectly efficient end state, knowledge of present and future conditions is complete and the coordination of plans is perfect. From this he reasons that, in the market process that characterizes the disequilibrated real world, all improvements in knowledge must also be coordinating. It is in this way that the inclusion of a perfectly coordinated end state, an element of closed endedness, may have distracted Kirzner's attention from important elements of the market process that do not neatly fit into the coordination framework.[6]

While knowledge and coordination go hand in hand in general equilibrium, they are not as neatly correlated in the disequilibrium world of the market process. In other words, while knowledge improvements may be equilibrating, in that, ceteris paribus, they move us closer to a world of "perfect knowledge," they may not always be strictly coordinating. Stories concerning an entrepreneurial process where general improvements in knowledge will take markets through different stages of discoordination and coordination can easily be told.

Imagine that widget entrepreneurs A and B from above are trading in a perfectly coordinated fashion in two separate markets. A is selling quantity $Q_a$ at price $P_a$ and this combination is completely consistent with A's plans and the plans of his customers. Widget seller B faces a similarly coordinated situation in his market at $P_b$, selling $Q_b$. But due to the lack of any knowledge that might connect the two markets $P_a<P_b$. Clearly gains from trade could be exploited if either A, a third entrepreneur, C, or the consumers in B's market gained knowledge of the price discrepancy. But this new knowledge and the exploitation of these gains would lead to at least a period of discoordination. This would be particularly true for entrepreneur B. But it may also be true for some of B's customers and for entrepreneur A, as output plans must be adjusted upward. Clearly, as market participants adjust to the new information, plans and goals will be reassessed and market activities will ultimately be recoordinated. But we cannot necessarily say that the newly coordinated environment is better than the old one.

Clearly, entrepreneur B may have been made worse off by this discovery of knowledge, even if eventually his new plans dovetail with the plans of a new set of market participants. If entrepreneur B is forced to go out of business, certain of his customers may end up having their plans disrupted and ultimately less fully coordinated. For example some inframarginal customers who were patronizing B out of loyalty or because of B's personal characteristics may have been willing to pay a higher price for B's widgets but their business alone was not enough to sustain the operation. The point is that this entire process, which Kirzner would certainly consider beneficial, has elements of both discoordination and coordination.[7] I will argue, in the chapter that follows, that the reasons why this entire process is efficiency enhancing is not because it is coordinating at every point in the process, but because it has lead to a situation where knowledge is being more fully utilized.

A second criticism of Kirzner's framework that deserves mention here, has been made, indirectly, by O'Driscoll and Rizzo (1985). Their focus is on the end state equilibrium that is implied by Kirzner's analysis. They have argued that Hayek's notion of coordination, which has been explicitly adopted by Kirzner (1988A), implies an equilibrium state that is both too restrictive to be useful in real world economic analysis and logically flawed. They argue that the level of coordination that is necessary for a general equilibrium end state requires not only ex ante plan coordination but also that all expectations concerning future events be consistent. They cite an example where one person sells an umbrella expecting that it will not rain tomorrow to a person who is expecting that it will. Ex ante, the plans of the buyer and seller are compatible and this is what gives rise to the exchange. But it is "logically impossible" for both parties to have their expectations fulfilled (O'Driscoll and Rizzo, p. 80).

Generally speaking, they argue that the perfect knowledge which is required if all exchanges were to be made on the basis of mutually consistent expectations is a logical impossibility (O'Driscoll and Rizzo, p. 84). But O'Driscoll and Rizzo go beyond the arguments being made here concerning the usefulness of general equilibrium as a tool of normative economics. They further question its usefulness for most predictive and explanatory purposes in economics (p. 114).

The extent to which O'Driscoll and Rizzo's arguments constitute a case against Kirzner's welfare economics is questionable. Kirzner himself has argued, on the one hand, that he considers comparisons between real world coordinating processes and nonreal-world end states to be irrelevant. On the other hand he has argued that a "perfectly efficient" world would be characterized by the end state equilibrium that O'Driscoll and Rizzo criticize (Kirzner, 1973, p. 218). Furthermore, O'Driscoll and Rizzo do not argue against the usefulness of some notion of relative plan coordination as a normative welfare standard. They do not challenge the notion that coordinating economic processes are always to be desired over discoordinating processes. They argue that the desirability of an economic system can be judged by the extent to which it allows individuals to adjust to the information changes that are inherent in the passage of time. With Kirzner, they relate this directly to the coordination of plans in arguing that:

> . . . we can assess [] the performance of an economic system on the basis of its adjustment to change. Here the criterion is the relative amount of coordination consistent with the system's exogenous change (O'Driscoll and Rizzo, p. 115).

O'Driscoll and Rizzo identify a coordination standard that is less restrictive than Kirzner's; they call it "pattern coordination." This standard allows them to focus on the likelihood, i.e., probability, of plans being fulfilled rather than on whether specific plans of specific individuals can be carried out. They conclude by arguing that "maximal possible [as opposed to complete] plan coordination is the most straightforward adaptation of the plan coordination concept to dynamic problems" (p. 118). Unfortunately, their discussion of "pattern coordination" is preliminary with no discussion of how it can be directly applied to concrete issues in welfare economics or how it would lead to analyses, either positive or normative, that are qualitatively different from a more Kirznerian approach to plan coordination.

Although Kirzner's coordination standard of efficiency has not been perfected, it is the most highly developed welfare standard in the Austrian literature. Unlike the criticisms leveled against Rothbard's demonstrated preference, most of those that have been made of Kirzner's standard are not so fundamental as to undermine the use of plan coordination as, at least, a partial benchmark for normative analysis. In light of this, Kirzner's standard offers a logical starting point from which to develop a more complete Austrian alternative to standard welfare economics.

## NOTES

1 Unlike Samuelson, Rothbard rejects the entire indifference curve framework for analyzing preferences and also rejects any assumption that preferences remain constant over time.

2 Rothbard has always been a strict advocate of a Lockean natural rights approach to private property. This implies a concept of voluntarism that is inextricably tied to the use of one's own body and "justly acquired" property (Rothbard, 1982b and 1973A).

3 The implications of Kirznerian efficiency theory for externalities were first discussed in Cordato, 1980, pp. 400-402.

4 Kirzner describes "utter ignorance" as a non-rational kind of ignorance. It does not refer to knowledge unaquired because the costs of acquisition are too high, i.e., rational ignorance. It refers to knowledge where no rational choice with respect to its acquisition can be made. It is knowledge that "you don't know you don't know." (Kirzner, 1986).

5 These, in the terminology of orthodox externalities theory, would be referred to as "pecuniary" externalities and are typically not considered Pareto relevant.

6 This discussion should not be interpreted as an indictment or rejection of general equilibrium in all economic analysis. My focus here is strictly on its use in normative, welfare economics.

7 Unlike High, I am making a distinction between coordination and equilibration. High, like Kirzner, associates the two, arguing that because the entrepreneurial process is both coordinating and discoordinating that it is therefore both equilibrating and disequilibrating. But since the entrepreneurial process is always knowledge enhancing, even though at different stages it may be discoordinating, my conclusion is Kirznerian in that, I believe entrepreneurship is always equilibrating but may not always be coordinating.

# 3

# CATALLACTIC EFFICIENCY: WELFARE ECONOMICS IN AN OPEN ENDED WORLD

## CATALLAXY AND ECONOMY

The arguments presented in the "Introduction" against efficiency and welfare economics stem from a concern that it has been constructed in the context of a fundamentally flawed vision of the world. Economists who are trying to assess the effectiveness of market activities confront a social phenomenon that is essentially different from the one depicted in the perfect competition model and the concept of social welfare that it has spawned. The essence of this difference is captured in the distinction, most consistently recognized in the works of Hayek (1976) and Mises (1966, pp. 232-234) (also see Buchanan, 1979B), between catallaxy and economy. Hayek has defined the distinction as follows:

> An economy . . . consists of a complex of activities by which a given set of means is allocated in accordance with a unitary plan among competing ends according to their relative importance. The market order serves no such single order of ends. What is commonly called a social or national economy is in this sense not a single economy but a network of many interlaced economies . . . [T]he cosmos of the market neither is nor could be governed by a single scale of ends; it serves the multiplicity of separate and incommensurable ends of all its separate members. (1976, p. 108)

Following Hayek, we adopt the term "catallaxy" to describe this vision of what is usually called the market economy. It is characterized by the fact that there is no overall hierarchy of ends that can be ranked on a single scale of values. The term "economy" applies only to individuals and those institutions, i.e., business enterprises, households, etc., within the catallaxy that do proceed from the perspective of ends ranked on a single ladder of importance.

In this setting there is no room for the notion of social welfare as it is typically construed. Social cost-benefit analysis implies a common scale of value upon which the decisions, and therefore the ends, of separate market participants can be ranked and compared in terms of a single objective--the maximization of net social benefit. In this context, the efficiency problem is one of allocating resources to their highest valued use, implying a single scale of values upon which comparisons can be made. This is the case with externalities. External effects, positive or negative, result in market failure because they prevent resources from flowing to their most highly valued use. As Hayek has pointed out though, this is a meaningless goal when cast within the context of a catallaxy. He argues that the catallaxy cannot "assure[] that the more important comes before the less important, for the simple reason that there can exist in such a system no single ordering of needs" (1976, p. 113). The notion of "economic efficiency," when implemented in a social setting, is inappropriately applied and therefore misconstrues the nature of the phenomena that is being judged. From the perspective of a catallaxy there are no social costs and benefits, per se, but only individual costs and benefits associated with the attainment of individually determined and ranked goals.

In assessing social welfare, economic efficiency, i.e., the efficiency of economies, has an important role, but only as a component of a more relevant notion which will be labeled "catallactic efficiency." Economic efficiency, in the strict sense of the term, applies to assessments of the means-ends framework of individuals and organizational units within the catallaxy. It is confined to addressing the question of the relative appropriateness of alternative means in the pursuit of a given hierarchy of ends. In the overall scheme of economic science, the concept of economic efficiency, finds its most appropriate place in certain subfields such as the theory of the firm and the theories of organizational and consumer behavior. The concept cannot logically be transplanted from the assessment of the activities of economies within the catallaxy to the catallaxy as a whole. This is what standard welfare economics has inappropriately done. It has lead to an obfuscation of the real social welfare problem that is faced by a market system.

## CATALLACTIC EFFICIENCY

Catallactic efficiency, by its very nature, is an expression of social efficiency. A catallaxy is a social order generated by the market activities of separate individuals and organizations, each pursuing their own purposes. A theory of catallactic efficiency should provide a framework from which this social order can be evaluated. It should provide a meaningful criteria that allows the economist to determine whether the system is working "better" or "worse" and that can give guidance in determining how the system can be improved.

In constructing a theory of catallactic efficiency we must be careful not to fall into the same trap that has snared the standard theory of economic efficiency. In other words our theory should capture the essence of the phenomenon that it is to pronounce judgement upon. The concept of catallaxy implies two important criteria for a theory of efficiency and ultimately, social welfare. First we need to start with the fact of individual autonomy. In other words, we must recognize, as outlined above, that we are dealing with a social order made up of individuals and organizations each pursuing their own, subjectively defined program of goals. This implies, first and foremost, that the theory should be what Hayek calls "ends independent" (1976, p. 36). In considering the question of efficiency the economist has no framework from which to pass judgement on the ends being pursued by market participants. As has been noted, there is no common hierarchy of values upon which to rank the different goals of all of society's participants. On a more fundamental level, since value rankings are determined intrapersonally, there is no way for an outside observer to discover any individual's ranking of goals or even the goals themselves. Economists, and therefore efficiency theory, have no choice but to abstract from the ends that are being pursued by market participants. Any attempt to pass judgement on particular ends for the purpose of determining either social or individual welfare cannot be considered scientific.

This signals an important and fundamental difference between economic efficiency and the theory of catallactic efficiency here under consideration. Implicit in more standard notions of efficiency, with the exception of a strict Paretian criteria of unanimity, is a judgement that some people's ends are more "valuable" to society than others. This conclusion can have no place in either a theory of catallactic efficiency or the normative analysis of externalities that it gives rise to.

A further implication of the notion of ends independence is that value must be viewed as inherently subjective. If there is no common scale of social value, and no way of knowing the value scales of any particular individual, there is no way to make interpersonal cost-benefit comparisons or even intrapersonal comparisons across time. As a guide to social welfare, such comparisons necessarily must pass judgement on competing ends and would automatically blur the distinction that is being made between catallactic and economic efficiency. Therefore, the two fundamental tenets of Austrian economics, methodological individualism and subjectivism, must be part of any operational theory of efficiency.

In conjunction with and as an implication of subjectivism, any analysis of people's preferences must be based on a recognition and acceptance of the guiding principle behind Rothbard's theory of social utility, i.e., revealed or "demonstrated" preference. Since the economist cannot project a value scale onto individual actors within the catallaxy, preferences can only be deduced by observing activities. Furthermore, since states of knowledge can and do change with the passage of time, preferences that are revealed at a point in time cannot be assumed to remain constant over time. Again, this is an important part of Rothbard's analysis that can and should be used as a building block for the theory presented here.

In addition to being "ends independent," which implies the conclusions just reached with regards to subjective value, the theory should be careful not to make assumptions concerning the amount of knowledge that is "given" to market participants. Certainly, an assumption of perfect knowledge would make no sense in this context, but beyond this, the idea that knowledge is "given" at all must be avoided. At the individual level, or the level of "economic efficiency," the acquisition of knowledge is the efficiency problem. This, as will be discussed in more detail below, is the most significant lesson in Kirzner's theory of efficiency. Rather than being viewed as a given, the level of knowledge must be considered the most important "variable" in the social order. This will be true for both the individual and the society as a whole.

**Economic Efficiency**

Any theory of catallactic efficiency must start with economic efficiency. In other words, the question must be asked, what constitutes efficiency for the individual actors that make up the catallaxy? In this regard, wholesale adoption of Kirzner's theory of efficiency for the individual is appropriate. It provides the necessary first building block for a theory of social or catallactic efficiency.

At no point can such a theory detach itself from the efficiency problem facing the individual. As has already been noted such detachments are part and parcel of more standard approaches to welfare economics. The most ironic example is found in the conclusions reached from a Pigouvian perspective when analyzing positive externalities. Even though, by definition, no one is made worse off as a result of external benefits that are generated in the production or sale of a good, "social welfare" is said to be reduced. From a different perspective, but still within conceptual framework of "economic" efficiency, Richard Posner, discussing the problem of negative externalities from a Coasean perspective, states that:

> The question whose cost is not a profitable one in economic analysis . . . The relevant question from the standpoint of economic analysis is who could prevent the loss at lower cost, not whose cost the damage 'really' is. (1973, p. 94)

Such dichotomies between the costs and benefits facing society and those facing the individual cannot be sustained in light of the catallactic perspective adopted here. Clearly the focus on ends independence and its implications for interpreting value as a purely personal and subjective phenomena preclude any such distinctions.

To review from the previous chapter, Kirzner starts with a view of man that might best be called "goal seeking," as opposed to the more standard "utility maximizing" homo economicus. For establishing a theory of catallactic efficiency, this distinction is important. Conceptually, it takes the actor out of the timeless framework of "utility functions," where ends and the perfect knowledge of means are a given. It also eliminates the temptation to illegitimately quantify utility functions and therefore combine them to form a social welfare function. Kirzner's vision is also the view of man embedded in Hayek's notion of catallaxy. Hayek's discussions consistently refers to the ranking of goals on individually determined value scales.

The efficiency problem in this setting is one of achieving the desired goal or set of goals by the most consistent use of means possible. For the individual, efficiency depends on the extent to which his actions, the means employed, are consistent with the goals or ends that are hoped to be accomplished. This is a "knowledge problem." The efficiency of an individual's activities will improve as he obtains more knowledge that is relevant to his particular situation.

Another way of viewing this is that the efficiency problem for the individual is the problem faced in formulating and executing plans. All plans are made with respect to actions that will be taken at future points in time. Since knowledge about the future cannot be perfect, varying levels of uncertainty will always pervade the formulation of plans. This perspective inextricably links catallactic efficiency to the passage of time and takes it out of the context of comparative statics.

Implicit in this discussion is the fact that in order for individuals to formulate plans and accomplish any goals they must have access to physical resources. The more appropriate the resources are for the accomplishment of the individual's goals, the more efficiently those goals will be obtained. Of course, this too is a question of knowledge. In order for any physical resource to be useful as means to an end, the user or potential user must first know that it exists. Beyond this he must have information concerning better and worse ways of obtaining it and then using it either by itself or in combination with other resources. The better this information, the more efficiently the resource will be used.

In the isolated context of individual efficiency, i.e., a Crusoe, the issue of obtaining or gaining control of the appropriate physical means is a personal one. It depends only on one's own physical abilities and knowledge. In a social setting, acquiring appropriate means becomes an interpersonal issue and needs to be a central focus of any theory of catallactic efficiency. For the moment it is important to note that in order for individuals to make plans and eventually achieve their goals they must be able to acquire both the appropriate knowledge and the appropriate physical resources.

Note that all of this is consistent with our stricture that no particular level of knowledge be assumed for the individual. It should be clear that the assumption of perfect knowledge in this setting would eliminate the problem entirely. If the individual, acting in a non-social setting had full knowledge of all the means available and how those means could best be used, the question of more or less appropriate means would be moot, and therefore the efficiency problem would not exist.

This suggests a point of contention with Kirzner's depiction of the efficiency framework within which the individual operates. While Kirzner does not assume any particular level of knowledge on the part of the actor, the concept of perfect knowledge does play a role in his theory. He postulates a condition of "perfect efficiency" where the actor has "perfect knowledge" in the sense described above. This is used as a foil against which the relative efficiency of an action can, conceptually, be judged. While I believe that the concept of perfect efficiency is unnecessary, at the level of the individual it makes little difference with regards to the nature of the efficiency problem. At most it would result in a quibble about whether the individual is striving to obtain the highest level of knowledge that is consistent with his means ends framework or is striving for something called perfect knowledge.

Conceptually though, perfect knowledge and therefore perfect efficiency, adds an element of "closed endedness" to the efficiency problem. Kirzner's theory, without the foil of perfect knowledge, is a more realistic portrayal of the world that individuals face. In reality, people in pursuit of their plans are always obtaining new information and discarding old. Value scales, and therefore programs of action, are always being revised in a never-ending process of trial and error. There is no end to this process, either in reality or conceptually. A crucial analytical departure from Kirzner comes at this point. The efficiency problem, i.e., the knowledge problem, for the individual is completely open-ended. This leads us to conclusions concerning the nature of social or catallactic efficiency, that are at odds with some of the most important of those that are reached by Kirzner.

**Social Welfare as Catallactic Efficiency**

> The economic problem of society is . . . a problem of how to secure the best use of resources known to any member of society, for ends whose relative importance only these individuals know . . . It is a problem of the utilization of knowledge . . .
>
> Hayek, 1945, pp. 77-78.

> Efficiency for a social system means the efficiency with which it permits its individual members to achieve their several goals.
>
> Kirzner, 1963, p. 35.

The efficiency of a catallaxy can be judged by the extent to which it promotes economic efficiency. In other words, it is to be judged by the extent to which the catallaxy encourages individuals existing in a social context, to pursue their own goals as consistently as possible. The individual is taken out of isolation and placed in a social setting described by the notion of catallaxy, i.e., where their are other individuals all pursuing their own, sometimes mutually incompatible, goals.

By its very nature, then, questions of catallactic efficiency must focus on the institutional setting in which individual actors operate. In particular there are two overriding issues. The first centers around the institutional setting that will best facilitate the use and discovery of information, the appropriateness and relevance of which can only be known by those who need to discover and use it. The second concerns the institutional setting that will allow individuals to gather the necessary physical resources. Here, the appropriateness and relevance of these resources can only be known by the person who is seeking them. As noted above, the resource and knowledge requirements are closely linked. The fact that a useful physical resource exists is meaningless until the knowledge of its existence and its relative usefulness are acquired.

Logically these questions might best be viewed in reverse order in which they have been presented here. The question of individual acquisition and use of resources in a social setting is crucial to the remainder of the analysis. In a fundamental sense, without access to physical resources all the knowledge in the world would be useless. In order for any individual to achieve his goals he must be able to make plans with respect to the use of resources and be reasonably confident that when the attempt is made to implement those plans that those resources will be available. In the case of the isolated individual, this concern would relate primarily to natural factors or personal carelessness that could lead to the destruction or alteration of resources that were being relied upon. But in a social setting, the problem of interpersonally conflicting plans with respect to the use of the same physical resource becomes an important consideration. When placed in a social setting, then, an additional problem concerning the efficient use of physical resources arises. Individual A can only be secure in his plans with respect to resource X if he is sure that individual B is not also making plans with respect to its utilization. In a social setting where different individuals are pursuing different ends, efficient resource use can only occur when conflicts in the use of resources are minimized.

This suggests that an important cornerstone of any institutional setting that is going to promote catallactic efficiency will have to be private property. The mere existence of a catallaxy is conditional upon individuals having rights to resources that they can then allocate in accordance with their program of goals. Without the ability, i.e., the right, to direct physical resources toward individually determined higher and lower valued uses, no goals could be pursued and no plans could be executed.

A corollary to private property, and following directly from it, is exchange. Exchange is the fundamental way in which individuals within a system of private property acquire relatively more appropriate means for the attainment of their ends. Indeed, an act of exchange is an act of giving up less appropriate means for more appropriate means. It is the dominant social mechanism for the promotion of economic or individual efficiency. Both parties to the exchange give up something that they consider to be less appropriate for the achievement of their ends for something that they see as more appropriate. In a catallaxy the fundamental way in which individuals pursue their goals is through the exchange process. Since all market exchanges are, at least ex ante, mutually beneficial, they also allow individuals to minimize conflict. This implies that catallactic efficiency must focus on the extent to which the exchange process facilitates the achievement of individually determined goals.

This reintroduces the issue of knowledge acquisition. In a social setting the better people are able to identify advantageous exchange opportunities the better they will be able to make plans, acquire more appropriate means, and pursue their goals more efficiently. In a catallaxy, the efficient pursuit of goals hinges on knowledge of exchange opportunities. The price system generates much of this information. In the most fundamental sense, the individual, by considering the array of product and price offerings that confront him, can discover those other individuals whose plans most consistently mesh with his own. Relative price and product comparisons give people information concerning what potential trading partners offer the most beneficial exchange possibilities.

Discrepancies between input prices and prices that can be received for final products, and generally unrecognized discrepancies among competing price offerings for the same product, inform alert entrepreneurs of profit opportunities. The possibility of earning these profits through arbitrage, provides entrepreneurs with the incentive to facilitate exchanges that otherwise would not be consummated (Kirzner, 1973).[1] Also movements in relative prices over time signal information about changes in people's preferences and the extent to which particular resources are becoming more or less scarce. These price changes inform individuals about how best to allocate their personal resources, including time and energies, in order to maximize their own exchange possibilities. These are just a few of the more general ways in which prices and price changes keep traders informed about the potential for more efficiently pursuing their goals through the exchange process.

A crucial efficiency concern facing a catallaxy is the problem of facilitating relatively more advantageous exchanges. The economist's role is to identify the institutional setting, legal and otherwise, that will best promote the pursuit of individual goals through the exchange process, i.e., institutions that will allow the price mechanism to bring to light and facilitate the most advantageous exchanges possible. The role of an economic policy analyst is to identify problems and virtues of public policy proposals in light of this efficiency concern.

## IDEAL INSTITUTIONAL SETTING VS. IDEAL MARKET OUTCOMES

The standard notion of economic efficiency, which focuses on a perfectly competitive general equilibrium, defines efficiency in terms of an ideal set of market outcomes--perfect knowledge, homogeneity of product, many firms, free entry and exit, etc. These give rise to the specific efficient outcome for any given market, namely a level of output that equates price, marginal private and social cost, and marginal private and social benefit.

It should be clear that in the open-ended setting of catallactic efficiency, specific outcomes of this nature cannot be preordained. Efficiency here is construed in terms of an open-ended process of pursuing goals, where people make mistakes, readjust their plans in light of new information, and continue on. It is inherently a process of trial and error, with no end-state of rest ever even considered by the participants in the process.

The task of the economist, when considering normative questions, is to identify those institutions that best facilitate this process. Within this context, an ideal institutional setting can be identified that serves a similar purpose to that of the conditions of perfect competition in standard welfare economics. This setting can be used as a benchmark against which real institutions can be judged and public policy proposals can be measured. The identification of this institutional setting will have no normative implications for particular activities or outcomes that occur within the context of that setting. In other words, there can be no judgments made about optimal output levels, the relationship between price and costs, the number of firms in a market, etc.. On the other hand, judgments can be made with regard to activities that operate outside of, or otherwise violate, the ideal institutional framework.

To reiterate, the overriding purpose of this ideal setting is to identify, generally speaking, the framework within which individuals, as social beings, are able to most efficiently pursue their goals. For reasons discussed above, it must incorporate the notion of private property as a fundamental starting point. No meaningful means ends framework is even possible without the ability to access and control physical resources. Beyond this, the role of this institutional setting is to allow the exchange process, through the price system, to disseminate as much information concerning appropriate exchange opportunities as possible.

The methodological rules that have been guiding this theory of catallactic efficiency generally, must also be incorporated into this ideal institutional setting. In particular, it should be "ends independent," with all that this implies concerning the subjective nature of value. Hayek stresses this point. In setting guidelines for public policy making within the context of a catallaxy he argues that:

> [policy should] be directed toward securing an abstract overall order of such character that it will secure for the members the best chance of achieving their different and largely unknown particular ends. The aim of the policy in such a society would have to be to increase . . . the chances for any unknown member of society of pursuing with success his equally unknown purposes. (Hayek, 1976, p. 114)

An important implication of this is that any institutional setting that hinges on interpersonal cost-benefit analysis is ruled out a priori. For example, a legal environment such as that envisioned by Coase (1960), particularly in a positive transactions cost world, would not fit these criterion. While stressing the importance of private property, Coase's world hinges on the ability to make interpersonal cost-benefit comparisons and therefore is not ends independent. (More will be said on this in chapter 5.)

Kirzner (1963) has set forth a general legal framework that is consistent with the goals of catallactic efficiency. His purpose was simply to state his own view of the "ideal" legal framework for the functioning of a society based on contract and exchange. According to Kirzner, this "ideal system may be thought of as, in one way or another, ensuring the smooth fulfillment of such cooperative arrangements" (1963, p. 14). Since his analytical concerns with respect to the individual planning process and the knowledge disseminating functions of the price system are the same as those being embraced here, the institutional setting that he describes is completely consistent with the concerns of catallactic efficiency. In Kirzner's words:

> In a market system each member of society is free to act, within very wide limits, as he sees fit. Moreover, the system operates within a framework of law which recognizes individual rights to property. This means that each individual is free at each moment to employ the means available to him for the purpose of furthering his own ends, providing only that this should not invade the property rights of others. (Kirzner, 1963, p. 13)

Kirzner first starts with a recognition of the importance of property rights. But he goes beyond this to describe, in a general sense, the nature and content of those rights. Specifically, there are three simple criteria that are general enough to act as a policy benchmark in dealing with a host of problems, including those associated with externalities.

1. Individuals should have rights to property, i.e., title to property should be held privately.

2. Property rights should take the form of allowing the individual "to employ the means available to him for the purpose of furthering his own ends."

3. In pursuing his own ends the individual is obliged "not [to] invade the property rights of others."

Number 1 simply establishes the principle of private property. Titles to property should be clearly delineated. As Hayek has stated:

> The chief function of rules . . . is to tell each what he can count upon, what material objects or services he can use for his purposes, and what is the range of action open to him . . . by making it possible to derive from ascertainable facts to whom things belong. (1976, p. 37)

Criteria 2 and 3, though, go on to delimit the rights that individuals should have with respect to their entitlements. Clearly these rights are very broad and are limited only by the same rights of others.

The important point is that these three criteria are completely consistent with principles of catallactic efficiency. First, private property is incorporated as the fundamental starting point. As has been already argued, no meaningful planning process could take place in the absence of rights to physical resources. Second, this legal setting is "ends independent." It emphasizes that people need to be allowed to use their property, both directly and through market exchange, in a way that is consistent with their own purposes. As a corollary to this, the single limitation on property usage (number 3) implicitly recognizes our concern that conflicts over the use of property, i.e., that two or more individuals may make incompatible plans with respect to the same property, can severely hinder the successful implementation of plans. Hence, property rights should be exclusive.

This institutional setting also has important implications for the exchange process and the effectiveness of the price system. Since it maximizes the extent to which the individual's own plans come to bear on the use of property, mutually agreed upon market prices will reflect as much information about market participants preferences, expectations, and perceptions of resource scarcities as possible. This means that businessmen and entrepreneurs who use prices as a guide to their activities will face incentives to pursue production activities that will coincide as closely as possible with the purposes of consumers.

A further efficiency enhancing property of this institutional setting is that it provides a great deal of certainty in individual decision making. This aides both the individual planning process and furthers the goal of knowledge dissemination through the exchange process and the price system. The individual planning process is not static. It is forward looking and takes place through time. Since plan formulation necessarily involves the use of property at different points in the future, certainty with respect to legal rights and obligations removes what could be an important source of error from decision making processes.

Expectations about the future are an integral part of plan formulation and the information reflected in prices. These expectations are always burdened with some degree of uncertainty, and, sometimes, turn out to be wrong. By providing a high degree of confidence with respect to legal rights and obligations this legal setting removes what could be an important contributor to the overall level of uncertainty in the decision making process. Plans can be made with respect to legally acquired property, knowing that the right to execute those plans at some point in the future will be upheld. Kirzner also emphasizes this point, stating that "each individual can plan his activities with the assurance provided by the law, first that the means available to him at any one time are secure against appropriation by others, and, then, that he will not be prevented by others from enjoying the fruits of his productive activities" (p. 13).

This has important implications with respect to the exchange process. People are willing to pay certain prices based on the services that they expect to receive from the purchased goods. This is the basis for consumer preferences that are ultimately transmitted through relative prices and price movements. To the extent that people receive the services that they expect, their plans are consistent with the ends being sought. If, once the good was purchased, the rights with respect to the use of that product were altered such that the expected services could not be fully realized, then both the purchaser(s) of the product and the price system would be adversely affected. Prices would have captured and disseminated these erroneous expectations, adversely affecting catallactic efficiency.

The institutional setting outlined here will maximize catallactic efficiency relative to any other institutional arrangement. To reiterate Kirzner's concern, it will maximize the efficiency by which the individual members of the social system will "achieve their several goals." It does this by guaranteeing people individual control over resources, thereby minimizing conflicts in the planning process; by giving people the maximum amount of freedom in making mutually satisfactory exchanges leading to the acquisition of more appropriate means; and by providing a foundation that will allow the price system to disseminate as much of the relevant information as possible.

## THE MEANING AND CAUSES OF INEFFICIENCY

As with efficiency, inefficiency is broken down into two categories, economic and catallactic. Economic inefficiency has reference to the internal consistency of the individual means-ends framework. Catallactic inefficiencies are the result of economic inefficiencies that impinge upon interpersonal relationships, particularly the process of exchange and the price system.

Because people are fallible, inefficiencies will always occur. As has been emphasized, the process of pursuing goals is inherently a process of trial and error. To the extent that errors are made in formulating and executing plans, inefficiencies will arise. Economic inefficiencies can arise because of misperceptions about the appropriateness of particular means to the ends being sought or because of misperceptions concerning future states of the world. Given individuals capable of learning from mistakes, the process of pursuing goals is inherently in continuous adjustment, proceeding from less to more efficient activities until the end being pursued is achieved.

Economic inefficiencies can generate problems for the catallaxy at large when exchange decision are made based on false beliefs. This is why actual market prices can never be "perfect." They are always capturing some erroneous information about both demand and supply that has been generated by the false perceptions of individual traders. Again, given the incentives generated by profits and losses, plans based on any erroneous information generated by prices will tend to be revised and decisions will be reversed. Because of the open-ended nature of catallaxy, though, this is a continuously unfolding process where new, false information is always being filtered out.

Inefficiencies of this nature are due to the inherent imperfection of human beings and are unavoidable. As such they can be categorized as "natural inefficiencies." These inefficiencies can never be eliminated and therefore are not policy relevant. For the purposes of normative economics it is more important to focus on the issue of what might best be called "institutional inefficiencies" (see Rizzo 1980A). These are inefficiencies that are generated by deviations from the "ideal" legal framework. They can arise because people are prevented in some way from fully utilizing their property or because rights to property are not clearly delineated. In the former case, the execution of formulated plans may be blocked or plans that could lead to a more complete fulfillment of goals may never be made. In the latter case, where title to property is not clearly established, the result may be interpersonal conflict over the use of property, conflict that can make it necessary for plans to be revised or abandoned.

To the extent that deviations or violations of the ideal institutional setting interfere with the process of contracting and exchange, catallactic inefficiencies will arise. Where existing rights to property are intruded upon, it is likely that exchanges have been made, possibly the property in question was purchased with the now foiled plans in mind. This can affect the information flows that are being provided by prices throughout the production chain. To the extent that the execution and realization of plans are prevented by abridgements of property rights, erroneous information with regards to expectations and preferences will be incorporated into prices. Furthermore, to the extent that production plans and entrepreneurial decisions are based on the erroneous aspect of these prices, they too will have to be revised.

In the case where titles to property are not clearly delineated, several inefficient results are possible. First, this could lead to separate and incompatible plans being made with respect to the same resource. In such cases conflicts can prevent or hinder the execution of plans. Again, this will have effects on the price system similar to those mentioned above. To the extent that these conflicting plans are incorporated into the exchange process, possibly through the purchase of complementary resources, prices will be reflecting both erroneous and conflicting expectations. A possible, but probably less likely, outcome is that the resource is completely unexploited because no one explicitly has the right to use it. In such a case the resource enters into no one's means-ends framework and makes no contribution to the attainment of anyone's goals. From a catallactic efficiency perspective, this would truly be a "wasted" resource. Furthermore, to the extent that the lack of rights to this resource prevents it from becoming the object of exchange, price signals concerning the scarcity of like resources and substitutes for this resource will be incorrect.

Of course this discussion of inefficiency impinges heavily on the issue of externalities. In the more standard Pigouvian and, later, Coasean literature, externalities are problematical because of the social inefficiencies they generate. Our task in the chapter to follow is to examine any catallactic inefficiencies that can be traced to externalities. The two theoretical issues that remain to be examined concern the kinds of externalities that are inefficient in the open-ended setting of catallaxy and the policy implications of such inefficiencies.

## CONCLUSION: CATALLACTIC EFFICIENCY, KIRZNER'S COORDINATION STANDARD AND ENTREPRENEURSHIP

This view of catallactic efficiency is, in a fundamental sense, Kirzner's standard of welfare economics without invoking interpersonal plan coordination as the normative goal. The problems that I see with coordination as a normative benchmark for welfare economics were outlined in the previous chapter. As was argued, where Professor Kirzner sees coordination as synonymous with improvements in information, I suggest that the knowledge improvement process often leads to disruptions in previously formulated plans and, at least temporarily, some discoordination. Furthermore, Kirzner adds an unnecessary aspect of closed endedness to his standard by invoking perfect knowledge and therefore perfect coordination as a way of defining "perfect efficiency." I believe that it is more fruitful and less distracting to focus strictly on improvements in knowledge and the elimination of error as the desired end in a catallactic process. But all of Kirzner's concerns with regards to the individual's means-ends framework and the ability of the price system to capture and disseminate accurate information are embraced within this theory of catallactic efficiency.

Furthermore, Kirzner's vision of the entrepreneur as arbitrager is crucial to a catallactically efficient process. From this perspective the essential social function of the entrepreneur is to facilitate exchanges. That is, to make possible exchanges that would not otherwise have occurred, leading to a more complete realization of goals. Every entrepreneurial act within the context of a catallactic process can be viewed in terms of the entrepreneur's ultimate social function as an exchange facilitator. Contrary to Kirzner's conclusions, I do not argue that these exchange facilitating acts are always coordinating. But this is part of the distinction between the efficiency benchmark presented here and Kirzner's standard.

Clearly this theory of catallactic efficiency owes a great deal to Professor Kirzner's pioneering work on both the nature of efficiency and the role of the entrepreneur. I see the theory presented here as simply an extension and refinement of his efforts.

## NOTE

1 Note that in this context the entrepreneur is seen as an exchange facilitator. This is the catallactic function of the entrepreneur and is different from the usual function as viewed through the eyes of an "economy." More typically the entrepreneur is seen as a resource allocator. This issue is discussed at greater length below.

# 4

# CATALLACTIC EFFICIENCY AND EXTERNALITIES

The framework of catallactic efficiency suggests a mode of analysis for assessing the welfare implications of externalities that differs significantly from the standard approach. Most importantly, the impact that any external effects have on particular market outcomes, i.e., prices or output levels, cannot be a deciding factor in determining the effects of the externality on market efficiency. In the context of catallactic efficiency there are no particular prices or output levels that can be deemed efficient or inefficient a priori, i.e., apart from the goal seeking activities that have generated them.

Within the framework of the ideal institutional setting (IIS) outlined in the previous chapter, prices and outputs will be as efficient as possible. But this conclusion is reached only as a derivative of the fact that the plans being made and executed and the exchanges being made as part of the means-acquisition process are as consistent as possible with the sought-after goals. Prices and outputs cannot be divorced from these actions.

With the identification of an institutional setting that maximizes efficient plan formulation and goal seeking, in both an autonomous and market setting, the role of public policy is to make the refinements in legal institutions that will bring them closer to the ideal. If deviations from the ideal are identified at the level of institutional analysis, efficiency can only be improved by refining the institutional setting. Because of the knowledge problems facing policy analysts in the context of an open-ended market process, it would be futile to tinker with the outcomes that have been generated by activities carried out within the framework of a flawed institutional setting. It would require information that could only be generated by the actual process of individual goal seeking within the guidelines of the efficient institutional setting. This, necessarily, is future information that has not yet been generated and thus does not yet exist.[1]

From the perspective of catallactic efficiency, then, the assessments of externality-related outcomes found in standard welfare economics are not only irrelevant but meaningless. Such assessments would be accurate only by chance, with no meaningful benchmark for verification, even ex post. For the economist or policy maker concerned about catallactic efficiency, the only way to improve market outcomes is to adjust the institutional setting in which plans are formulated.

## EXTERNALITIES AND SOCIAL EFFICIENCY

The relative social efficiency of any activity that gives rise to externalities can only be judged by the extent to which it distorts the knowledge generating and disseminating function of the catallaxy. That function is distorted when people are prevented from making and executing plans that they otherwise would be able to make, and accurate information concerning preferences, scarcities, expectations, etc., is prevented from entering the exchange process. If an externality gives rise to such problems it will hinder the efficiency of individual goal-seeking activities. Conversely, if the externality does not have such effects then it cannot be judged detrimental. External effects that enhance goal-seeking activities, then, should be seen as promoting efficiency. Within this framework the term "externality" does not automatically have negative connotations. It is possible that some externalities considered detrimental to social welfare in the traditional Pigouvian framework could enhance goal-seeking activity and therefore promote catallactic efficiency.

By using the IIS as a guide, the efficiency properties of certain broad categories of externalities can be evaluated a priori. With respect to the negative consequences of goal-seeking activities, the social welfare effects of externalities can be deduced by examining the extent to which they result in, or are a result of, deviations from the ideal. More concretely, the IIS dictates that not only should property rights be clearly defined and strictly enforced, but that the fullest latitude possible, consistent with the same rights of others,[2] be given with respect to the use of all entitlements. To the extent that an external effect is inconsistent with this property rights framework, it can be judged inefficient.

### Positive and Negative Externalities

In examining externalities within the framework of catallactic efficiency the standard definitions and categories may be adopted. The concepts of positive and negative externalities as received from standard Pigouvian analysis are suitable as broad categories of external effects, but in and of themselves they have no unambiguous normative implications. Further refinements of the "positive-negative" framework need to be made. Each of these categories can be broken down into those external effects that are consistent with the IIS and those that are not. The diagram below can be a useful guide.

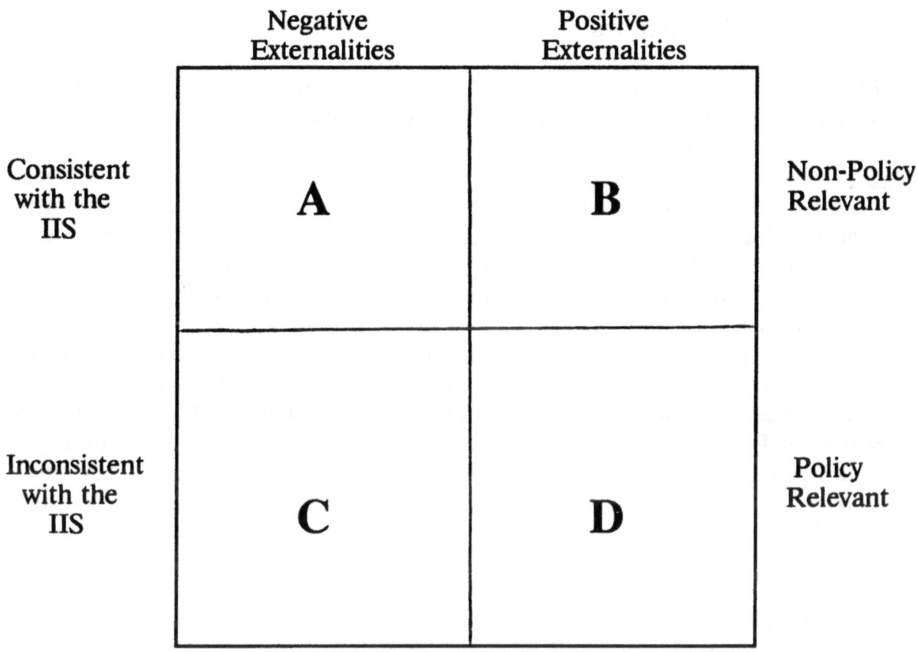


Those externalities that fall into the lower half of the matrix can be analyzed as unambiguously generating efficiency problems for the catallaxy. Furthermore, at least conceptually these externalities can be dealt with through some refinement of the institutional setting. Thus, they can be categorized as "policy relevant." In other words, the possibility exists that efficiency can be enhanced through some public-policy action.

Those that fall into quadrants A and B will need further refinement in order to reach some specific conclusions concerning their implications for catallactic efficiency. But as will be demonstrated, any problems that are caused by externalities that lie in this half of the matrix cannot be unambiguously improved on by exogenous manipulation of either market results or the institutional setting. Any unambiguous improvements in efficiency with respect to externality problems that arise in these two categories must be generated endogenously through market activity. It will be argued that these external effects should not be the target of public policy and they will be categorized as "non-policy relevant."

**Policy-Relevant Externalities**

By their very nature, externalities that are inconsistent with the IIS are most likely to be negative, i.e., those that would fall in quadrant C. I will leave open the possibility that quadrant D could be empty. (An exception might be those positive externalities that are associated with intellectual pursuits and new inventions. These will be discussed below.) In particular we are considering externalities that involve the physical invasion of property rights or those that involve a conflict in the use of property to which title is not clearly defined. The former is a problem of property rights enforcement while the latter is a matter of ambiguity in property rights.

This is not to argue that it is impossible for positive externalities to be the result of uninvited physical invasions of property. For example, one could imagine a classical music fan living next door to a concert violinist, where, happily, the sound of the violinist's practicing drifts into the neighbor's surroundings. While this positive externality, at least initially, represents the use of one's property by another without his permission, it ultimately turns out to be a "welcome" intrusion and therefore does not constitute a violation of the IIS. For a policy-relevant externality problem to exist, it must first physically invade the rights of others or make use of property that the person generating it is not clearly entitled to. Second, it must, in an unwanted manner, interfere with the formulation and execution of plans with respect to the property that is being coopted. If the second criterion is not met, there can be no negative impact on catallactic efficiency. The positive externality generated by the violinist does not meet that second criterion.

Most of the standard cases of negative externalities, such as air, water, and noise pollution, fit into the category represented by quadrant C. These would be interpersonal conflicts over the use of property, conflicts that prevent plans made with respect to that property from being carried out. Those are unambiguous "externality problems," and conceptually, if not always practically, they can be remedied by making refinements in the legal-institutional environment such that it more closely conforms to the IIS.

The problems associated with these externalities result from one of two kinds of deviations from the policy bench mark established by the IIS. The first, and most straightforward, is the direct invasion of one person's property by another. A simple example was invoked by Coase (1960): cattle belonging to rancher A crosses onto farmer B's land, destroying his crops. In this case all property titles are clearly defined and the problem is one of enforcement. The catallactic efficiency problems that arise are clear. The farmer has made plans with respect to the use of his property that, because of the actions of the rancher (more specifically, his cattle), he is prevented from carrying out.[3]

Furthermore, this will have implications for the relative accuracy of information that is being captured and disseminated through the price system. It is likely that contracts were made based on the expectation that the destroyed crops would eventually come to market. In light of the externality, the contracted prices have captured false information with regard to the relative scarcity of the farmer's product; that in turn has sent and is sending false signals to other market participants.

The solution is to enforce the farmer's right to use his entitlement as he sees fit, thus restoring the conditions of the IIS. (The specifics of that kind of solution will be discussed in the following chapter.) In terms of public policy, only this solution would unambiguously enhance catallactic efficiency. It could be argued that to do nothing and allow the property rights invasion to continue, i.e., to effectively transfer rights for the purposes of grazing to the rancher, could also restore catallactic efficiency in the long run. In other words, the farmer's expectations and plans, and therefore market prices would adjust to the new property rights arrangement.

While that may be true in a strictly static setting where the problem at hand is viewed in isolation, this kind of solution would have a detrimental effect on the plan formulation process in general. Ultimately it would introduce a great deal of uncertainty with respect to property rights themselves. People acquire property with purposes in mind. As discussed, to make efficient plans, and by implication for prices to project accurate information, people need to be able to count on having the right to use that property for their purposes. If people cannot be sure that their property rights will be upheld the whole process of plan formulation and goal seeking in general would be severely hampered. Risks associated with the possibility of not being able to eventually implement some plans could prevent what would otherwise be mutually beneficial exchanges from being made and ultimately could prevent many goals from being achieved or even pursued. As will be noted in the following chapter, this creates efficiency problems for the negligence rule in tort law that are typically ignored in the standard analysis (see Rizzo, 1980A).

A second kind of problem that could arise as a policy-relevant externality is associated with ambiguity in entitlements. Imagine an unowned or "publicly owned" stream that is being polluted, making it unusable for recreational purposes by residents downstream. A conflict has arisen because of ambiguities with respect to entitlements to the stream. Two separate sets of plans have been made with respect to the same physical resource. This can be traced to a flaw in the existing institutional setting, i.e., property rights are not clearly defined.

From the perspective of public policy the problem could be resolved by clearly delineating entitlements to either the entire stream or different portions of it and then enforcing those entitlements,[4] i.e., by forcing conformity to the IIS. But this leaves open the question of how the decision should be made. It brings us face to face with the issue of how to decide who should have title to property that is not clearly owned by anyone. A lengthy discussion of this issue here would be tangential to the primary purpose of this chapter, which is to delineate those kinds of externalities that are problematical within a context of catallactic efficiency. Specific solutions to these kinds of problems as they arise within the context of tort and nuisance law are discussed in the next chapter. On the other hand, it is appropriate here to deal with certain theoretical issues that arise at this juncture.

The standard approaches to dealing with the issue of original entitlements are theoretically flawed, from the perspective of both Austrian economics and catallactic efficiency, and have no practical value as real world guides to policy. Typically those approaches involve methodologically illegitimate and fundamentally non-operational interpersonal utility comparisons, and consequently are not ends-independent.

Coase's analysis (1960) (to be discussed at greater length in chapter 5) suggests that the rights to the stream should go to the person whose use adds most to the social value of output. But both subjective value theory and the knowledge problem suggest that this approach is not only non-operational, but more fundamentally, that Coase's normative standard, i.e., maximizing the social value of output, has no meaningful economic content.

This is not to suggest that a "Coase theorem" type solution, where the problem is resolved by mutual consent that arises through a bargaining process, would be unacceptable. In fact, this would, from the perspective of catallactic efficiency, be the most promising solution. But no conclusion could be reached regarding the relative "social value" of output that results from this bargaining process. Furthermore, in the absence of a bargain, that solution could not be mimicked by a judge or other public policy maker, as is suggested by Coase and assumed in most of the law and economics literature.

Buchanan's constitutional approach, which focuses on rules determination and property rights arrangements before market processes are set in motion, i.e., in a state of nature (1975), also offers no practical public policy guide for problems such as those that arise with the unowned stream. Buchanan focuses on the unanimous agreement that could be reached with regard to undetermined entitlements when individuals are trapped behind a Rawlsian-type veil of ignorance. But clearly that is not the world that is being dealt with when analyzing day-to-day externality problems. As noted, unanimous agreement among the affected parties, possibly brought about as part of a bargaining process, would be ideal. But the relevant public policy question must focus on how to delineate property rights in the absence of mutual consent.

The Pigouvian approach, for the same reasons that apply to Coase, also offers no solution to this problem. As noted, the Pigouvian solution requires the objectivisation of costs and benefits and the use of interpersonal utility comparisons. But the problem of defining property rights would still need to be resolved if Pigouvian tax policies were to be implemented. The basic question of who is the source of the problem and therefore who should be taxed cannot be determined in the absence of property rights. This is the problem of joint causation implied by Coase's article (1960) and this was a central theme of Coase's criticism of Pigou's analysis. The Pigouvian approach is essentially institutionless. In any given conflict, who has title to what resources must be assumed before Pigouvian analysis can proceed. This is as true for public goods problems as it is for negative externality problems (see below).

Given the intractable problems facing the standard approaches to this issue, Austrian economists have argued that the question of defining property rights crosses the boundaries of economics as a science. Nearly all Austrians have seen that issue as an ethical question beyond the scope of economic analysis (Egger, 1979; Rothbard, 1979; Kirzner, 1979).[5] Moreover some have argued that such questions must be resolved before economic analysis can even begin. O'Driscoll and Rizzo reflect the typical Austrian view in stating that "the basic questions of right and wrong, of the justice of entitlements . . . must be resolved before economic reasoning can be used in policy analysis" (p. 118).

To some extent we can question the typical agnosticism of Austrians, qua economists, on the issue of original entitlements. We have already shown that there is a role for economic analysis when analyzing the implications of "unowned" property for externality problems. In the stream pollution example, prior to determining the "justice of entitlements," economic reasoning can be invoked to describe the detrimental effects that such a situation can have on catallactic efficiency. Furthermore, such reasoning can be used to suggest the appropriate focus for public policy. Prior to settling the ethical issue of who should be granted the entitlement in question, it is possible to use economic analysis to point out the efficiency problems that will arise from such a situation and to delineate the outlines of a policy solution. Taking this analysis one step further, it will be argued in the following chapter that economic analysis, again invoking a standard of catallactic efficiency, can be used, in some situations of tort, to settle the final question of who should get the entitlement.

I am not taking issue with the entire thrust of the more traditional Austrian conclusions in this area. While the approach here suggests that in some instances economic analysis can be useful in helping to decide questions of original entitlement, this is not true in all cases. The general Austrian approach, even with catallactic efficiency as a backdrop, severely limits the extent to which economic reasoning, particularly costs-benefit analysis, can be used to resolve externality problems where property titles are not clearly defined. A completed public policy approach to this issue needs not only a theory of efficiency, but a theory of justice. Economists who do not recognize this lack a clear understanding of the boundaries of economic science and, as is often the case, are bound to espouse incoherent and inappropriate approaches to public policy.

Before moving on to the issue of externalities that arise within the context of the IIS, those in the upper half of the matrix, we need to examine the possibility of policy-relevant externality problems that are the result of the generation of external benefits. In other words, externalities that would fall into quadrant D. As was argued above, positive externalities by definition do not result in the violation of anyone's property rights. If they are truly positive externalities they become a welcome "intrusion" from the perspective of the recipient of the external benefit. For this reason, it could be argued that, quadrant D is empty, i.e., there are no policy relevant external benefit problems. (The issue of whether externality problems or efficiency analysis in general is appropriately used as a justification for establishing institutions for formulating and instituting policy in the first place will be discussed later in this chapter and in the conclusion of this book. This is the question of whether the typically perceived positive externality problems associated with public goods, i.e., free rider problems and joint consumption problems, can be used ultimately as a justification for the existence of a government. For our purposes here, it is assumed that an apparatus of some kind is in place for adjudicating and enforcing property rights disputes.)

Mises has suggested, though, that an external benefit "problem" might arise where intellectual property rights are not clearly defined; this is the issue of patents and copyrights (see chapter 1). Mises clearly focuses on an issue of property rights that may have normative implications for catallactic efficiency. Ambiguities with respect to entitlements in the area of inventions and the generation of ideas can lead to interpersonal conflicts in the plan-formulation and goal-seeking process. As noted, to efficiently make plans, individuals need to know that their rights to use the relevant property will be upheld at pertinent points in the future. The issue of patents and copyrights may be an application of this principle.

On the other hand, this is clearly an area where the limitations of economic analysis are exposed and a theory of justice may need to be invoked. Consistent with O'Driscoll and Rizzo's point, this is a case where certain ethical questions need to be resolved before economic analysis can be applied. The question of whether property rights can legitimately be applied to ideas, particularly given that ideas and inventions can be and often are independently discovered, has both practical and ethical implications. In such cases, the granting of property rights to a discovery itself denies the rights of others who have made or will make the same discovery independently (Rothbard 1970, p. 71). This denial of rights would clearly interfere with plans that were made by the independent discoverer and may consequently have a negative impact on the accuracy of some market prices. This suggests that the granting of property rights to ideas would likely lead to its own problems with respect to catallactic efficiency.[6] Mises's brief analysis, providing neither a theory of justice nor efficiency, does not give us a satisfactory approach to this issue.

As discussed in Chapter 1, Rothbard rejects the notion of intellectual property rights, noting the conflicts that arise with respect to the rights of independent discoverers. He also points out that, if reproduction is the concern, the inventor of a product or the writer of a book can, through contract, limit the rights of others with respect to the use of these products. Furthermore he rejects the standard external benefits argument for intellectual property rights which claims that the lack of such rights results in the underproduction of research and innovation. Invoking the standard Austrian criticism of orthodox externalities analysis, Rothbard asks, "By what standard do you judge that research expenditures are 'too much,' 'too little,' or just about enough?" (1970, p. 72).

If it is concluded that discoveries and ideas are not the appropriate target of property rights then these kinds of externalities would be moved to quadrant B in the upper half of our matrix. In other words they would not constitute a violation of the IIS. That may be the appropriate positioning for such externalities in any case, since it is not clear that catallactic efficiency is unambiguously improved by establishing such entitlements, particularly given the problem of independent discovery. Clearly this issue is one of many that would require further analysis within the context of this theory of externalities. The purpose of this book is not to thoroughly analyze and resolve every issue that can arise under the rubric of externalities, but to provide a general framework under which that analysis can proceed.

As an aside, it should be pointed out that the absence of clearly defined property rights in ideas and inventions has not proven to be a market-paralyzing problem. There are many areas where patent and copyright protections do not exist and production flourishes. These include fashions, management and marketing strategies, scientific principles and mathematical formulae, and artistic endeavors such as comedy, magic, and jazz improvisation.[7]

### Non-Policy-Relevant Externalities

Non-policy relevant externalities are those external effects that, while possibly effecting the utility level of the recipient of the externality, is neither the result of or results in a violation of the IIS. Such externalities can be either positive or negative. Furthermore, while often such externalities will impinge on the plan-formulation process, i.e, they will not necessarily be neutral with respect to people's means-ends framework, they will not have the effect of distorting price signals. In other words, the accuracy of information flows associated with prices will be unaffected. The hallmark of that kind of externality is that catallactic efficiency cannot be unambiguously improved on through public policy.

Most negative externalities, even in the standard literature, involve the invasion of one person's property by another. But there are examples where negative externalities are generated completely within the context of clearly defined and well-enforced property rights. In chapter 1 we discussed the case of neighborhood effects. For example, the person who stores old cars on his front lawn may impose a negative externality with respect to both his neighbor's utility level and possibly the value of his neighbor's property.

First, it should be pointed out that from a strictly subjectivist perspective, the presence of such externalities would be unverifiable by an outside observer, such as a policy maker or economist. There is no way of telling what the actual impact of such an effect is on the utility of those living in the neighborhood; no way of knowing whether such effects are necessarily negative. For example, other old car enthusiasts or automobile hobbyists in the neighborhood may find such circumstances aesthetically pleasing. For them the cars on their neighbor's lawn could represent a positive externality. Furthermore, even if utility were observable, in cases where the cars might be generating both positive and negative effects, there is no way of telling, since utility is not comparable, whether, on net, they represent a positive or negative externality.

Similar conclusions can be reached with respect to the effect of the externality on the market value of homes in the area. Others who are inclined to store old cars on their front lawn may actually be willing to pay more to live in a location where they have neighbors who are doing the same thing. To know the effect on the market value of homes in the area, one would have to know what the value would be in the absence of the externality--clearly an impossibility.

Even if they could be independently confirmed as positive or negative, from the perspective of catallactic efficiency such externalities are simply not a problem. At the individual level they do not interfere with plan-formulation or implementation. There is nothing the neighbor cannot do with his property in the presence of the externality that he could do in its absence. Clearly, the external effect may have an influence on his plans. If the cars on his neighbor's lawn do indeed reduce the market value of his property, he may alter plans that have been made with respect to selling it. But the notion that the price that can be gotten for the house with no cars on the neighbor's lawn is the "correct" price is arbitrary and ultimately meaningless. All prices are determined, to some degree, by factors that are "external" to the particular item being sold. To argue that the influence of some of these "external factors" are appropriate while others are not, simply substitutes the values of the economist for the values of the market participants. To suggest that the outcome should be altered by public policy is to suggest that people have a "right" to a particular price for items they wish to offer for sale. If this were the case, any market based system would quickly retreat into chaos.[8]

At the market level there is no interference with the knowledge gathering and dissemination function of the price system. While such effects may have an impact on prices, that impact will not be distorted. The market price of houses in the neighborhood will capture accurate information about preferences and expectations. There is no reason to expect that such externalities would cause the price system to capture false information or send misleading signals to market participants. It is the standard Pigouvian solution to this "problem" that would give rise to inefficiencies. Any attempt to force the "internalization" of the externality through a curtailment of property rights, assuming that the externality could be appropriately identified, would interject inconsistencies into plans that the externality-generating neighbor has made with respect to the use of his property. In general this would prevent the full utilization of his property for the achievement of his goals.[9] Furthermore, any Pigouvian-type tax in such a situation would have to be viewed as nothing more than an arbitrarily imposed excise tax. Outside of the analytical framework of general equilibrium, the efficiency properties of such a tax would fall away. In fact, given the problems of determining the net effects of the externality, it would be impossible to know whether to impose a tax or to grant a subsidy.

With regards to positive externalities, it might be useful to invoke Mises's two categories discussed in chapter 1. A type 1 external benefit is one where, in spite of the externality, the good in question continues to be produced. This is analogous to what the standard literature would consider a less than purely public good. A type 2 external benefit is one that renders the good in question unprofitable to produce at all and is analogous to a pure public good.

From the perspective of catallactic efficiency, there is no reason to judge either outcome as inefficient. Catallactic efficiency offers no benchmark from which to judge any output level as "too much" or "too little." A type 1 external benefit would be analogous to the practicing violinist discussed above. If one wanted to put this in terms of a good being produced for marketing, we could look at the relationship between an outdoor concert and those who might live adjacent to the concert site. (Assuming that this were indeed a positive externality for those living nearby.)[10] In terms of catallactic efficiency it is irrelevant that if these people could be forced to pay for the concert, more concerts would be held. No plans are being disrupted, and no rights are being violated. Furthermore, there is nothing inherent in this situation that would distort the signaling mechanism of prices. Prices could be expected to capture as accurate information as possible concerning people's demonstrated preferences given the presence of the externality, and the costs, including transaction costs, associated with internalizing the external benefits.[11]

As has been traditionally the case with Austrian analysis, a type 2 externality result may be an interesting one from the perspective of positive economics, in that it represents a particular kind of explanation of why a good might go unproduced in a market. But the result itself has no normative implications. A production level of zero is no less optimal than any positive level of production. In fact, so long as that outcome reflects a market process that was the result of decisions made within the context of the IIS, the process and therefore the outcome would have to be judged efficient.

From the perspective of catallactic efficiency and the Austrian school in general, the only time a type 2 outcome could be deemed inefficient is ex post, and then only by the market participants themselves. If this turned out to be the case then it would be expected that the market process would modify itself in the direction of a more efficient, i.e., means-ends consistent, outcome.

The results that Mises associates with this type of externality are essentially the results that are gotten in the case of a "pure public good." Because of a severe free-rider problem, no profits can be generated from the production of the good and therefore the good is not produced. But if this result is shown, ex post, to be inefficient from the point of view of market participants, then we can expect behavior to be modified and a tendency will exist to convert this situation into a type 1 externality. All that would be necessary to convert a type 2 result into a type 1 result is that the good become profitable to produce. If the goal of market participants is to obtain the good and they realize that their means, i.e., free riding, is inconsistent with their ends, then continued attempts at being a free rider would be irrational.

Not all potential market participants would have to change their actions for this type of conversion to take place. What would be necessary is simply that enough individuals decide that they want to achieve their end badly enough to pay an amount sufficient to create a profit opportunity for potential entrepreneurs, in spite of the fact that positive externalities will be generated. As long as there are people who are actually willing to pay a profit-generating price to obtain the good, a true opportunity for mutually beneficial exchange will arise. If a consumer's goal is not strictly to obtain the good for free, it would be irrational for him to continue his inefficient behavior once he learns that the good is not forthcoming.

According to what Kirzner describes as the "market discovery process" (1985, p. 137), just such a learning process can be expected. Kirzner argues that:

> [d]emand for regulation . . . stem[s] from the belief that unsatisfactory conditions will never be corrected unless by deliberate intervention. Such demands . . . might be muted . . . were it understood that genuine inefficiencies can be relied upon in the future to generate market processes for their own correction . . . the urge to . . . alter [market] outcomes must presume not only that these undesirable conditions are attributable to the absence of regulation, but also that the removal of such conditions cannot be expected from the future course of unregulated market events. (1985, p. 137-138)

It is not being argued that all type 2 externalities will eventually evolve into type 1 externalities only that those type 2 externality results caused by the inefficient pursuit of goals should eventually make the conversion. If the good continues to go unproduced, it must be assumed that people will demand it only if they can obtain it for free, or at least at a price insufficient to generate a profit. If this is the case, then, as argued above, the result cannot be appraised as inefficient.

This discussion assumes that the process and results being discussed are occurring within a context where property rights are recognized and enforced. In other words, it cannot be said that goods that go unproduced as a result of free-rider problems within that context should be produced. The question arises as to the production and maintenance of the institutional setting itself. What if the institutional setting goes undeveloped as a result of free-rider problems? This is the typical argument for state provision of courts and protection services such as police and national defense. It is argued that such institutions would not arise in the absence of coercive measures instituted by a state.

In fact, though, this is ultimately a discussion of a good that may go unproduced outside a market setting. In other words, in order to establish markets there must be a system of recognized property rights. Any discussion of markets or catallactics assumes the right to trade. To argue that the institutional setting necessary for a market to exist will go unproduced in a free market is putting the cart before the horse. This is ultimately a question of how to establish and maintain, in a prior sense, the institutions that are necessary for the existence of catallactic processes.

The discussion here can tell us what the role of those institutions should be once they are established, namely to delineate and enforce property rights according to the guidelines of the IIS. What a theory of catallactic efficiency cannot do is dictate how those institutions should be established and maintained in the first place. Such a discussion, by definition, comes prior to the beginning of catallactic processes. That point is typically ignored in the standard analysis of the public goods question.

The underlying and unstated assumption in standard public goods theory is that people have the right to make certain trades but choose not to make them. In order for orthodox analysis to proceed with respect to analyzing the provision of those institutions that establish and protect property rights, such as courts and police protection, it must assume that the very institutions that the market supposedly is failing to produce already exist. It is illogical to argue that markets would fail to produce the institutions necessary to establish and protect property rights when these institutions are a necessary pre-condition to having markets. If people do not already have rights to exchange, at the very least, their labor services, and to control and exchange the fruits of those services, the fact that an exchange process does not develop in such a way as to give rise to those rights cannot be legitimately called a "market failure". Certainly to argue that the necessary institutional setting is a pure public good that would go unproduced by markets is to place one in a logical contradiction. The right to contract and make exchanges is necessarily inherent in all market analysis, including Pigouvian public goods analysis.

That issue is finessed even in Buchanan's discussion of how rules of the game would be established by unanimous consent in bringing society out of a Hobbesian state of nature. As with public goods analysis, the underlying and unstated assumption is that people, at least, own themselves and have a right, presumably enforceable, to make contracts.

Ultimately, this issue which is typically addressed as a part of welfare economics and leads to the economic justification for the existence of government, is not a question of economic or catallactic analysis at all. Such issues must be dealt with before invoking economic analysis. Some argue that such institutions as police and courts would, and historically did, in some settings, evolve spontaneously without the existence of an organized state apparatus (see Rothbard, 1973; Friedman, 1973; and Benson, 1990). Whether or not such institutions would flourish without invoking coercive elements, such as taxation, through a state apparatus is an empirical question open to debate. Furthermore, whether it is worth using, at the margin, such coercive measures in order to obtain more property rights protection than would occur in their absence is also debatable. Economics, along with other social sciences such as sociology, anthropology, and history can be used in a positive sense to inform those debates. Catallactic efficiency can provide a normative justification, in a general sense, for the establishment and maintenance of private property rights, but economics must remain agnostic from a normative perspective with respect to the question of how the institutions meant to establish and maintain those rights are initially created.

Similar analysis applies to the appropriate level of property rights protection. Assuming that the appropriate institutions are in place, normative questions related to the tradeoffs that "should" be made between additional protection or refinements in the institutions and other goals, public or private, cannot be directly answered through efficiency analysis. To the extent that such decisions are made through the state apparatus, economics can help clarify some of the opportunity costs associated with transferring additional resources from the private to the public sector, and some of the benefits that might accrue for the market process as the result of enhanced property rights enforcement. The relationship between those costs and benefits cannot be weighed by the economist to determine an "optimal" level of enforcement. This issue would have to be solved through the political process.

The same would be true if the issue were determined through completely voluntary means. Efficiency analysis could not be invoked by an economist or other third party to determine whether the level of property rights protection that is being chosen is "optimal." At the margin, people would decide, based on their own perceptions of costs and benefits, the level of property rights protection that is consistent with their other goals. Clearly, this is the case now for those who desire and purchase property rights protection over and above the level that is provided by the state.

The fact that the solution to these problems are not forthcoming within the context of catallactic efficiency is not a deficiency in the analysis relative to the standard approach. These questions are only apparently answered in the Pigouvian framework. As has been argued elsewhere, the tools that are typically invoked to determine the "optimal" level of national defense or police protection are fundamentally and irreparably flawed. The answers to these questions that Pigouvian analysis provides are, in reality, no answers at all. I agree with the traditional Austrian assessment in such areas: namely that an economist, qua economist, cannot offer a normative foundation for answering such questions. Ultimately other disciplines, in particular, philosophy and ethics, possibly informed by economic analysis, must provide the normative framework for assessing these issues.

## KIRZNER'S IIS: THE THREAD THAT BINDS

It is clear that the normative analysis of externalities in this chapter, invoking the welfare standard of catallactic efficiency, is consistent with the dominant Austrian approach of Mises and Rothbard. Furthermore the conclusions are the same as those that were reached when viewing the issue from the perspective of either Rothbard's demonstrated preference standard or Kirzner's coordination standard of social welfare. That agreement can be traced to certain fundamental concerns and presuppositions that all three of these approaches to efficiency and social welfare have in common.

First, there is the general acceptance of the proposition that efficiency or economic welfare can only be improved by altering the institutional environment in which the market must operate.[12] In other words, given the proper institutional setting, market processes, and therefore market outcomes, will be as efficient as possible. Once a set of ideal institutional conditions are satisfied, both Kirzner and Rothbard argue that no alterations of particular market outcomes can unambiguously improve efficiency or social welfare.

Beyond this though, there is a fundamental agreement on the specifics of an appropriate legal setting. It is this agreement that has led to the normative interpretation of externalities that most Austrian economists hold in common, even in the absence of a consensus on welfare theory itself. All three approaches to efficiency ultimately conclude, either explicitly or, as in Rothbard's case, implicitly through ethical analysis, that the most efficient legal arrangement for society is the one that is described by the IIS. After defining the market system as ideally coinciding with the legal environment established by the IIS, Kirzner concludes that interference with the market so defined can only decrease efficiency. He states that "interference with the . . . market process limits the attempts of participants to coordinate their activities through an engine of remarkable efficiency--the market" (1963, p. 309). Likewise, Rothbard, arguing from the perspective of "demonstrated preference" concludes that, "No government interference with exchanges can ever increase social utility . . . whenever government forces anyone to make an exchange which he would not have made, this person loses in utility as a result of the coercion" (1977, p. 29).

It would be inappropriate to conclude that those Austrian approaches to welfare economics have simply been ex post rationalizations for some ideologically desired result. It is arguable that these conclusions regarding institutional efficiency are an inevitable consequence of consistently following the constraints imposed by Austrian methodology. The consistent focus on individual goal seeking, a theme of Austrian analysis beginning with Menger, coupled with the analytical constraints of radical subjectivism, may necessarily lead to the IIS, or something close to it, as an institutional touchstone for normative analysis.

More specifically, Austrian methodology requires that any approach to normative economics take individual goals, preferences, and therefore perceptions of opportunity costs as given. An implication is that the analysis would have to be "ends independent" and eschew all interpersonal and intertemporal cost-benefit analysis. This methodological approach necessarily shifts the focus from comparative "outcomes" analysis to comparative "processes" analysis. More specifically, it leads to comparisons of the market processes that will arise under alternative institutional arrangements.

In this context, the concept of "market failure" has no meaning. The ability of the market system to promote efficiency from any of the Austrian perspectives is always limited by the institutional setting that it must operate within. The price system will capture and disseminate as much of the relevant information as that setting allows. The emphasis here shifts from the concept of market failure to the concept of "institutions failure."

All three of the approaches to welfare economics discussed here attempt, more or less successfully, to stay within the methodological guidelines of Austrian economics. From this perspective, any institutional arrangement that must consider the relative importance of different individuals' ends for its maintenance or general operation would have to be rejected. Furthermore, the emphasis on individual autonomy implies that any "ideal" institutional arrangement would have to allow the greatest possible latitude for individual goal seeking.[13] It seems that, given these constraints, the IIS will be the logical outcome of any comparative institutions analysis done from an Austrian perspective, regardless of the specific definition of efficiency guiding the analyst.

When externalities are viewed in light of the IIS the Austrian conclusions as originally put forth by Mises are automatically implied. Only externality "problems" that involve the conflicting use of property are inconsistent with that institutional arrangement. Activities that generate external benefits do not typically involve a conflict in the use of property and in general do not violate the ideal institutional conditions. Therefore, they are not seen as adversely affecting economic efficiency or welfare. The point is that the general normative analysis of externalities found throughout the Austrian literature can be interpreted as an attempt to establish or maintain a widely agreed on "ideal" institutional arrangement. In addition, viewing the analysis from this perspective gives it an overall coherency that cannot be seen when discussing it strictly from the perspective of any of the separate welfare criteria.

## NOTES

1 This highlights the profundity of the knowledge problem in operationalizing standard welfare economics. The results of any current assessment of prices and outputs could only be implemented at some point in the future. Information concerning preferences and therefore opportunity costs only becomes real as it is demonstrated through goal-seeking activities. Hence to make conclusions about efficient prices and outputs that relate to points in the future one must have access to information that does not yet exist. The knowledge problem is not just the very formidable one of gathering information that is out there but is also hopelessly diffuse. It suggests that the efficient manipulation of market outcomes requires speculation about the infinite amount of information that has yet to come into existence.

2 This point refers to the third criterion in the IIS (see previous chapter). In some sense it is redundant once it is assumed that property rights are clearly defined and strictly enforced.

3 The issue of causality will be discussed in Chapter 5 within the context of a theory of torts. But within the framework of the IIS the problem of joint causality (see Kelman, 1987 ) is not an issue.

4 For a discussion of how the practical problems associated with assigning property rights in such cases might be handled, see Anderson and Leal, 1991.

5 For ethical perspectives on how such issues may be handled, see Kirzner, 1979 (Chapter 12) and 1989, and also Nozick (1974).

6 It should be noted that often the problems that patents and copyrights address are and have been resolved through contract. Books and products can easily be sold with the stipulation that they not be reproduced.

7 See Palmer (1989) p. 287.

8 Contractual agreements to resolve such issues, such as protective covenants, are completely consistent with both the IIS and catallactic efficiency.

9 This analysis does not apply in cases where such rights are freely given up through protective covenants. Indeed, to give up rights to one's property in such a way, through contract, is itself a way of exercising those rights.

10 If this were a negative externality for some neighbors, it would be located in quadrant C and be policy-relevant.

11 If all such costs were included in calculations in the Pigouvian framework, there would be no way of arguing that such externalities gave rise to inefficient results. Inefficiencies arise in Pigouvian analysis only when transactions costs are subtracted from costs curves. (see Coase 1960 and Mishan 1973, p. 90)

12 This approach to welfare economics is not unique to Austrian economists. Coase (1960) and Buchanan (1975) have both adopted institutional analysis in discussing issues of welfare economics. In turn their work has given rise to entire fields of economic analysis (law and economics and constitutional economics, respectively) that examine the relative efficiency of alternative institutions.

13 This emphasis is ultimately derived from the concern that economists must not impose their values on the subjects of their analysis, what Mises called wertfreiheit (1966, p. 882-883).

# 5

## APPLICATION: THE ECONOMICS OF TORT LIABILITY

At first glance, the economics of tort law, as it has developed in the Coasean tradition, appears to be an area of analysis that is, in large part, consistent with the Austrian alternative presented here. In his 1960 article "The Problem of Social Cost," Coase, like the Austrians, was critical of Pigouvian analysis for ignoring the importance of property rights in both assessing the social consequences of harmful effects and in formulating public policy remedies. Furthermore by stressing the role of opportunity costs, Coase touched upon themes that have always been associated with the Austrian school. In fact, Buchanan (1981 & 1969) places the approach taken by Coase squarely within a mode of analysis that, he argues, was initiated by Hayek's 1937 article, "Economics and Knowledge." Finally, in a general sense, both the "Coaseans," in areas such as environmental economics and law and economics, and the Austrians have consistently advocated market-based, as opposed to centralized, solutions to economic problems. Recognizing this, Farrell (1987) presented and criticized Coase's 1960 article and Hayek's "The Use of Knowledge in Society" as completely consistent arguments for the decentralized decision-making of a market economy.[1]

In spite of these similarities between Coase and the Austrians, the approach to externalities and harmful effects developed here implies a significant reformulation of the way problems in tort law are assessed and ultimately dealt with. The methodological problems that Austrians have had with Pigouvian analysis also apply to both the economics of tort law as it has developed in the Chicago school tradition and to its underpinnings as they were first developed by Coase. In other words, while Coase's analysis rightfully took issue with Pigou, and has been cast in opposition to Pigouvian welfare economics, Austrian analysis takes both Pigou and Coase to task for similar reasons (see Cordato, 1989).

The primary purpose of this chapter is to illustrate how catallactic efficiency and the externalities analysis that it suggests can be applied to a particular area of analysis, the economics of tort law. Since this field of study has developed out of a non-Pigouvian property rights approach to the problem of externalities, it is important to clarify why it is not acceptable from an Austrian perspective. Before reconsidering the economics of tort law, a critical assessment of both the Coasean foundations of law and economics and its applications, as developed by Posner, Polinski, Priest, and others, is in order.

## COASE AND MODERN LAW AND ECONOMICS

Nearly all of modern law and economics, and particularly the economics of tort and contract, has been developed as a direct application of the theory presented in "The Problem of Social Cost" and in particular the "Coase theorem." All of the major textbooks in law and economics (Posner, Polinski) present Coase's 1960 article as the analytical touchstone for this entire field of study. It is important then to assess these widely recognized foundations. The problems that Austrian economists have had with the modern economics of tort law go directly to its foundations in Coase.

### Coase and Negative Externalities: A Problem of Social Cost

The primary concern of Coase's 1960 article was to reassess the normative implications of negative externalities. He argued that the traditional Pigouvian approach misconstrued the externality problem as a divergence between private and social costs. Furthermore, he concluded that this misperception could lead to less-than-optimal results in terms of the application of public policy. For Coase the traditional focus on the internalization of negative externalities was misplaced. He argued that the goal of public policy should be to maximize the value of output (p. 16), which may or may not imply the internalization of all harmful effects. For example, in considering the case of a factory contaminating a stream and killing the fish, Coase argues that the principle "question that needs to be decided is: is the value of the fish lost less than or greater than the value of the product which the contamination of the stream makes possible" (p. 27).

It should be clear, even before delving into the specifics of Coase's analysis, that there is a fundamental incongruence between Coase and the Austrians. The "question that needs to be decided" from Coase's perspective, is one that, for Austrians, is not only undecidable but essentially meaningless to ask. The subjective nature of value precludes from the outset any scientific comparison between the "value" of the lost fish and the value of the product that would have to be sacrificed in order to save the fish. For Coase this is clearly a problem of comparing and minimizing the opportunity costs to society associated with losing one kind of output or another. For reasons stressed throughout this book, it is the kind of normative standard that, from the perspective of catallaxy, could never get off the ground, even within the context of a zero transaction costs world (see Littlechild, 1978).

Coase highlights his alternative to Pigouvian analysis with many examples where the actions of one person or business has harmful effects on others. These problems are assessed within the context of one of two broad assumptions about transaction costs. His first scenario assesses the results that are obtained when transactions costs are zero or so low as not to hinder bargaining between the affected parties. The parties, regardless of who is held to bear the costs ex ante, will bargain their way to a result that will minimize the combined value of the products they are producing. This entire process has come to be known as the Coase theorem.

To demonstrate this result he uses the example of a cattle owner's herd straying onto a neighboring farmer's land and damaging crops. With zero transaction costs the self-interest of the farmer and cattle owner leads to bargaining that ultimately gives rise to the efficient result. This bargaining is based on the market prices of the farmer's crops, the cattle owner's beef, and the fencing that would be required to contain the cattle. Ultimately, side payments are made by either the farmer to the cattle owner, in order to obtain a reduction in the size of the herd, or from the cattle owner to the farmer, in order to obtain rights to a portion of the farmer's land, i.e. a reduction in the amount of crops planted. The direction of the side payments depends on who, prior to any bargaining, expects to have to bear the damage costs. In either case the bargaining results in the combination of crops and cattle that maximizes their combined social value. A critical assumption in Coase's analysis is that all prices are competitive equilibrium prices and therefore capture the marginal social costs associated with the productive activities involved.[2] This allows Coase to argue that both the market value and the "social" value of the two products are being maximized.

In the second and more relevant case, high transaction costs prevent the efficient result from occurring as a consequence of free bargaining. Under these circumstances a third party, likely to be a judge attempting to resolve a legal dispute, would have the task of determining "the arrangement of rights [that] may bring about a greater value of production than any other" (p. 16).

Coase uses an example where the sparks that are thrown off by a railroad set fire to crops that are growing near the tracks. For our purposes there is no need to go into the quantitative specifics of Coase's example (see pp. 30-31). Generally, the judge must examine the values, given by market prices, of the marginal outputs that are forgone in assigning rights to the railroad to destroy adjacent farmland, as compared to upholding the farmer's right to grow crops on that land. He must then use these calculations to determine which rights arrangement would maximize net social product. At this point, property rights, if necessary, are reassigned according to this maximizing rule.

The positive transaction costs scenario has become the foundation for most of the subsequent applications of Coasean analysis in the law and economics literature. Efficiency assessments of alternative liability rules in areas as diverse as automobile accidents and industrial pollution are, in a fundamental sense, specific applications of the general principles established in Coase's railroad vs. farmer example (see Polinsky, 1983).

As in the zero transaction costs case, in order to obtain the value-maximizing result, Coase assumes that all observed market prices are competitive equilibrium prices (p. 32). This means that, for the policy maker, the observed prices capture all of the relevant information that is necessary to determine the efficient solution.[3]

## From Coase to the Economics of Tort Law

> "What has to be decided is whether the gain from preventing the harm is greater than the loss which would be suffered elsewhere as a result of stopping the action which produces the harm." (Coase. p. 27)

In the literature assessing the economics of tort law, Coase's words capture the essence of what has become the judge's marching orders. The judge's role is to mimic the Coase theorem results. The Coasean standard has been adopted throughout the law and economics literature as the social norm that should be promoted by an efficiency-conscious judge and jury. In terms of alternative liability rules, this kind of analysis has led to a variety of policy conclusions, depending on the approach to assessing costs and benefits. Depending on the circumstances surrounding the tortious activity and the way in which the particular analyst formulates costs and benefits, Coasean-type efficiency cases have been made for strict liability, with and without a defense of contributory negligence, negligence only, and no liability at all.[4]

The most well known expositor of law and economics in the Coasean tradition, Richard Posner, generally argues in favor of some form of negligence approach to torts, including the possibility of a strict liability rule that allows for a defense of contributory negligence (see Posner, 1973). The problems of cost-benefit analysis as it is typically used to assess the efficiency of alternative liability rules can all be illustrated by examining the simplest approach to determining negligence, as invoked by Posner. More extravagant formulations of the efficiency problem, which in certain circumstances lead to support for rules other than negligence, suffer from the same fundamental problems associated with the simple rule discussed here. Therefore, there is no need to consider any of the more complicated alternatives found throughout the law and economics literature.

The economic concept of negligence has been defined in what is essentially Coasean terms.

> [T]he defendant is guilty of negligence if the loss caused by the accident . . . exceeds the burden of the precautions that the defendant might have taken to avert it . . . . If a larger cost could have been avoided by incurring a smaller cost, efficiency requires that the smaller cost be incurred. (Posner, 1973, p. 69)

This is formalized in what has come to be known as the "Hand formula."[5] The formula itself, invoked as an extremely general guide for the efficiency maximizing judge, holds that a defendant should be found guilty of negligence if $PL>B$, where P is the probability that a loss will occur, L is the value associated with the loss, and B is the burden or cost associated with preventing the loss.[6]

To reiterate, the economic analysis of tort clearly gets much more complex than the simple analysis suggested by the Hand formula. Furthermore, no one working in this area would suggest that applying the formula or the efficiency rule in general is, in the vast majority of cases, either simple or straightforward. But the Austrian criticisms of the standard economic analysis of tort are fundamental. The more complicated analyses in the law and economics literature are still all, in one form or another, applications of Coase's efficiency criteria. The problems that Austrian analysis has with modern law and economics stem from criticisms that are associated with its foundations. As such they apply with equal force to both its simple and more complex applications.

## SUBJECTIVE VALUE, INFORMATION, AND TIME: THE AUSTRIAN CRITIQUE

From an Austrian perspective, the problems that face a judge attempting to implement a Coasean-type solution are so fundamental as to make the entire procedure non-operational. The arguments that were made in opposition to the Pigouvian tax assessor are equally applicable to the Coasean judge (see the "Introduction"). But while the arguments are the same, the emphasis is slightly different. Both Coase and those who have applied the Coase theorem to problems in tort law, have, in their analysis, swept away the problems of subjective value, knowledge, and time passage by making one simplifying assumption: all observed prices are perfectly competitive prices. In other words, the analysis assumes away all the real-world public policy problems associated with our living not in a world of comparative statics but rather in an open-ended world of trial and error processes. The assumption that all decision making is based on perfectly competitive prices is not merely a simplification made in order to focus on a problem at hand; it is an essential ingredient. The normative conclusions that are associated with Coasean policy prescriptions could not be reached without this "simplification."

### Open Endedness and Coasean Analysis

> To assume all knowledge to be given . . . is to assume the problem away and to disregard everything that is important and significant in the real world . . . . [W]hen it comes to the point where [general equilibrium] misleads some of our leading thinkers into believing that the situation which it describes has direct relevance to the solution of practical

> problems, it is high time that we remember that it does not deal with the social process at all. [Hayek, 1948 (1945A), p. 91]

While Hayek's comments were directed at Schumpeter, it is clear that Coase and many of his disciples have been "misled" into a similar analytical trap. We can examine Coase's conclusions from a more realistic starting point. If we assume a catallactic process where prices are imperfect reflections of the relevant information and where the information that is generated is always being amended, both the Coase theorem and the more general Coasean approach to property-rights analysis run into intractable difficulties. Although, the implications for the zero transaction costs case are less drastic than for the more realistic positive transactions cost scenario.

Returning to the case of the cattle owner and the farmer, the assumption of zero transaction costs assures that bargaining will take place and that a mutually satisfactory result will follow. But if we do not assume that the market prices of the cattle and the crops involved are reflecting all of the relevant information, we are not assured that the bargained-for result will maximize the net social value of output.[7]

The best that can be said is that the result will maximize the market value of the cattle and the crops for the moment that the bargain is struck. Furthermore, even this conclusion depends on our assuming that there are no non-pecuniary factors that enter into the bargaining process. Without the assumption that prices are capturing marginal social costs, no conclusion can be reached concerning the net social value of the cattle and crops that are ultimately produced.

This conclusion, while not obtaining all of the results that the Coase theorem yields, does have normative implications that are significant from the perspective of catallaxy. First, it still can be concluded, in the absence of insurmountable transaction costs, that a mutually satisfactory outcome will be obtained. Even though it cannot be concluded that this result will maximize the net social value of the products involved, it is a result that leaves both the farmer and the cattle owner better off than they would be in the absence of the bargain. Left intact, then, is Coase's observation that in a zero or negligible transaction costs world, no outside intervention would be needed to resolve disputes concerning conflicts in the use of resources, so long as the right to bargain is guaranteed.

The implications of a disequilibrium world view for the positive transaction costs case and most of its subsequent applications are much more serious. In the absence of equilibrium prices, the amount of information that would be required of a judge (or any third party) in tort cases would create an insurmountable obstacle to obtaining the efficient, i.e. Coasean, solution. Clearly, if the Coase theorem results, in terms of social efficiency, are not unambiguously obtained in the zero transaction costs world, they cannot be mimicked by a judge trying to hammer out a solution in a positive transaction costs setting.

The problems can be highlighted by using Coase's simple example of the railroad and the farmer's crops. The problem faced by the judge is to determine whether the damage that would be incurred from crop-destroying sparks if two rather than one train per day was in operation would outweigh the value of the additional train service. If we place the judge within the context of a dynamic market process, where prices are not perfectly competitive, his problems become insurmountable. First, as an exogenous observer, he must decide whether the resource allocation that would result from non-interference, in this case the running of two trains per day, is suboptimal. If it is, he must then decide what the optimal allocation of resources is and whether or not any compensation for damages should be paid. To carry out the first task he would have to know all the opportunity costs associated with the use of the relevant resources for the point in time that the market is being observed.[8] The judge would then have to make the appropriate calculations needed to determine if the value of the "social product" could be increased by an alternative use of resources.

These first steps would need to be taken before any judgments could be made. Given that outside of competitive equilibrium all opportunity costs are subjectively defined and inherently unknowable, the Coasean judge would face an impossible task from the start. In other words, P, L, & B of the Hand formula, i.e., the information necessary to implement the negligence rule, are all conceptually unknowable.

But even if those obstacles created by the subjective nature of opportunity costs and the knowledge problem were possible to overcome, and a rational decision could be made to reallocate resources, the judge's problems would continue. In a dynamic market setting he would need perfect foresight with regard to all of the variables that were considered in his initial market assessment. As disequilibrium market processes unfold through time, utility functions and relative scarcities will change and opportunity costs will continuously fluctuate.

Outside the stable framework of competitive equilibrium, any judge attempting to reallocate resources and property rights according to Coasean guidelines would face a continuing set of obstacles. He would have to determine an appropriate time frame and obtain all the relevant knowledge, which is not captured in market prices, for making accurate present value calculations with respect to the resources involved. Furthermore, there is no logical conclusion to this process. Even in making the unrealistic assumption that a judge could obtain all the relevant information for a finite period into the future but not infinitely into the future, it would seem that he would have to continuously reconsider decisions at the end of each time period.

The purpose of this discussion is to highlight the fact that, from the perspective of a catallaxy that is always in disequilibrium, change is continuous, costs and benefits are subjective, and knowledge is inherently imperfect. In this setting a Coasean judge faces an impossible task. He must have access to accurate knowledge concerning the forgone opportunities associated with the use of the resources under consideration. Yet disequilibrium prices will not accurately convey this information. In fact, apart from preferences that are actually demonstrated, knowledge of costs and benefits is, in principle, unconveyable.

Furthermore, at a given point in time there is no way of telling how accurate the information that prices are conveying actually is. In other words, to argue that market prices are "close enough" to general equilibrium prices to be useful in this judicial decision-making process is an unverifiable assertion. To know this would be to already know the equilibrium price configuration. This would mean that all of the relevant information is at hand, even with out the use of market prices.

In this regard it is important to digress for a moment and focus on the judicial process described by Priest (1977) (see also Rubin, 1977, and Goodman, 1978). At first glance, it could be concluded that his work addresses the criticisms of standard analysis that arise from the perspective presented in this book. He argues that while every decision in the common law might not be efficient, the common law process encourages the legal system to promulgate increasingly more efficient rules over time (see also Rubin). Again, the distinction is between analysis that is carried out within the context of an open-ended market process that is characterized by a continuous flow of new information, and analysis that is carried out with a particular "efficient" allocative outcome in mind. Priest makes it clear that his analysis is Coasean (p. 66), i.e., efficient rules are those that result in an allocation of resources that would maximize the value of output (minimize "social cost"). In contrast with the open-ended catallactic process, he envisions a closed-ended system with particular market outcomes in mind.

His purpose is to explain why common-law rules can be expected to become allocatively more efficient over time, even if judges are unconcerned about the efficiency effects of their decisions. Priest describes a process of rule evolution that is driven by the amount of litigation that a particular rule generates. He argues that because inefficient rules will generate higher (joint) costs to litigants, they will tend to be relitigated more frequently. This increases the probability that they will be overturned in favor of more efficient rules. Priest describes an iterative process driven by the amount of litigation that a rule generates, which leads to an equilibrium solution dominated by efficient rules.

I am not arguing that there is a problem with this kind of analysis within the methodological framework established by Coase.[9] But Priest's analysis can be used as a vehicle for highlighting the differences between the Coasean and Austrian traditions. While Priest is describing a disequilibrium process, the focus is firmly fixed on the general equilibrium end state, which, implicitly, is part of the ceteris paribus conditions. But in a truly disequilibrium world where the end state is a continuously moving target, it does not make sense for legal rulings to attempt to insure <u>any</u> particular market outcome or distribution of resources. The allocatively "efficient" outcome, if it can be meaningfully identified at all, is likely to be different at each successive point, implying that it would only be by accident if any rule even tended toward "efficiency" by the time it was actually implemented. Subjective value theory causes further complications. In the framework adopted by Priest, the summing of costs and benefits across individuals, and comparisons of costs and benefits among individuals, are integral parts of simply defining efficient outcomes, and therefore efficient legal rules.

While those who have attempted to assess the efficiency of the common law, are, on one level, focussing on a judicial process that is in disequilibrium, the analysis is ultimately end state bound. From the perspective of catallactics, it is the Coasean welfare standard of "economic" efficiency that must be jettisoned from the analysis of tort law, including economic assessments of the common law.

## CATALLACTIC EFFICIENCY AND THE ECONOMICS OF TORT LAW

The problem of unintentional torts is a problem of negative externalities involving a conflict in the use of property. As such, the theory of catallactic efficiency can be directly applied. In doing so, efficient legal rules can be identified and alternative applications can be considered. The purpose here is to reconsider some fundamental questions in the economics of tort law to illustrate the theory developed in the previous sections. Hopefully this discussion will also serve as a foundation for further refinements and developments in this area. Ultimately, I believe that most questions in law and economics can be reconsidered from the perspective of catallactic efficiency. While a comprehensive analysis of such issues is well beyond the scope of this chapter, the theory presented here can form the basis for research into the history and evolution of the common law, the meaning of causation (touched on briefly below), contract law, antitrust law, and even criminal law.

Most problems in tort stem from the fact that there has been an interpersonal conflict over the use of property. Issues in both nuisance and accident law can be viewed from this perspective. The normative economic question that arises relates to the approach that judges should take in attempting to resolve such conflicts. What principles should guide judges who are attempting to maximize catallactic efficiency? What approach to rule making do these principles evoke?

Clearly, the overriding guidepost must be the notion that property rights should be clearly defined and, ultimately, strictly enforced. Ideally, a judge's rulings should be crafted, where possible, within the framework of the IIS. Where this institutional arrangement is not in place, the goal of the judge should be to improve the legal setting in the direction of the ideal. This suggests a fundamental difference in approach from the Coaseans. While in Coasean analysis property rights are viewed as the most important variable, from the perspective of catallactic efficiency, they must be taken as a given. If title to the property that is under conflict is clearly delineated, then the judge has no bases in efficiency from which to alter the existing rights arrangement. In cases where titles are not clearly delineated, the purely cost-benefit approach of Coase cannot be invoked to solve the problem. A different, and in many cases, a non-economic, ethical approach must be invoked.

The theory presented here leads to a non-Pigouvian efficiency defense of strict liability. We can illustrate the fundamental issue by examining Coase's railroad and farmer example in light of catallactic efficiency considerations. The application is straightforward. The principle question that a judge must ask in resolving this dispute is not whether the farmer or the railroad contributes more to the social value of output, but who owns the land that is acting as a receptacle for the sparks. Note that in Coase's analysis this is an unimportant question. In the zero transactions cost case it makes no difference who is the owner of the property at the time that the harmful effect is generated. The same efficient result will ultimately come about. In the positive transactions cost case, the task of the judge is to decide who should have the property rights, not who does have the property rights.

The approach presented here completely changes the nature of the judge's inquiry. Rather than focussing on the expert testimony of economists, presenting sophisticated cost-benefit analysis, the focus might more appropriately be on the results of land surveys and the nature of deeds or contractual arrangements such as protective covenants. In the case at hand, if the farmer had title to the land that the crops were growing on, there is no question that his right to continue to grow them should be upheld. The railroad should be held strictly liable for the damage inflicted. Possibly, it should be forced to internalize the sparks, for example, by building a fire wall. This would be an issue of injunction versus damage relief, clearly an area for further research from this perspective. The point is that, in accordance with the IIS, the farmer should be allowed to fully utilize his property in a way that is consistent with his hierarchy of ends. On the other hand, if it were determined that the framer's crops were being grown on land owned by the railroad, then the right of the railroad to incinerate as much of it as it pleases should be upheld. In either case, at least in a prima facie sense, the judgment should be for whoever has title to the property.

It should be pointed out that the purpose of a strict liability rule in this case is not Pigouvian. The internalization of costs, per se, is not what gives rise to the efficiency. The point is that it is a rule that strictly enforces property rights. It is consistent with the IIS, and therefore, if predictably applied, it will enhance the efficiency of both non-social and market oriented goal-seeking activity. Precise calculations of external costs are not a necessary ingredient.

The concept of strict liability being advocated here has been most extensively developed by Richard Epstein (1973, 1974, 1975), and has typically been endorsed by Austrian school economists (Rizzo 1980A&B; Rothbard, 1982 and Lewin, 1982). But for the most part, this support has been grounded in ethical considerations or what Epstein refers to as "corrective" justice (1979), and has been as an outgrowth of rejecting Coasean-type efficiency considerations (see Egger, 1979; Rizzo, 1980C; and O'Driscoll and Rizzo, 1985). The conclusion that has typically been reached is that efficiency is not an appropriate guide for such questions. As O'Driscoll and Rizzo have argued:

> Our support of [judicial rectification of tortious acts] . . . rests on a belief in principles of corrective justice. We would not pretend that utility is being maximized by the use of common law remedies. We would be quite pleased, however, if the victim were made whole. Pursuit of the latter strikes us as a worthy enough goal even if it falls short of [a] . . . welfare ideal that is . . . unattainable in principle. (p. 142)

This concept of strict liability should be distinguished from the concept that is currently being invoked in the debates concerning tort reform and products liability. In that setting the concept is associated with the nearly complete abandonment of contract and the idea that the plaintiff should never bear the costs of his or her actions. As it is currently being used in discussions of products liability, "strict liability" negates any attempt to limit liability through ex ante agreements between buyers and sellers. Indeed, this approach to liability is inconsistent with catallactic efficiency. It interferes with the contracting process, i.e., voluntary exchange, and therefore denies people the full utilization of their property. It is an approach to liability that limits and, in fact, denies certain property rights with respect to contract. There is no question of who owns what, or what rights and liability limitations have been agreed to as part of the contracting process. I believe that the term "absolute liability" rather than strict liability is more an appropriate term for the approach to consumer products issues that has developed over the last several decades (Huber, 1988, ).

## The Question of Causation

Strict liability, as endorsed here, is rooted in the notion of property rights and, as such, suggests a concept of causation that is similarly centered around property. As has often been pointed out, the implementation of strict liability requires an approach to the issue of causation (Kelman). Rizzo sees causation as an integral part of the definition of strict liability. He argues that:

> A system of strict liability . . . is preeminently based on causation. A is liable, at least prima facie, if he is the cause of B's harm. (1980B, p. xi)

In the standard framework established by Coase, it is typically argued that the concept of causation is vacuous. This view has been succinctly summarized as follows:

> [T]he injury cannot have occurred unless the plaintiff (P), at a minimum, *existed*, that is P is invariably a necessary condition for the damage to occur, we can never causally attribute any injury solely to a second party, a defendant (D). It will never be the case that the injury could occur

> without the plaintiff, such that the defendant is entirely causally responsible .... [W]e can never fully causally attribute damage to any D, and there is no obvious way to distinguish, on purely causal grounds, the relative causal contribution of two wholly necessary parties .... [this is] the most basic Coasean insight that parties *interact* to cause harm ... (Kelman, p. 579)

The Coasean perspective on causation is the result of totally divorcing this concept from the existing arrangement of property titles and rights. While the Coasean paradigm focuses on the analysis of property rights, the central question is always who should have the rights, rather than who does have the rights.[10] From the perspective of negligence, the economic analysis suggests that each case should start out as a blank slate in terms of property rights. This is consistent with the Hand formula, which is completely agnostic on the question of rights and ownership at the time of the accident or tortious act. From this perspective, then, not only is all harm in tort jointly caused, but the question of causation is ultimately unimportant.

As opposed to Coasean analysis, where property rights are the most important variable, the Austrian school's approach to all externality related issues has consistently been that clearly delineated property titles and rights must be taken as given. The notion of strict liability that is derived from that view of property rights casts up a "but for" test of causality that subverts these conceptual ambiguities. Causality is established, at least prima facie, if, but for the fact that the plaintiff (P) invaded the property rights of the defendant (D), the harm would not have occurred. In this case "invade the property rights" means to make use of property that D had title to, without D's permission.

In the case of the railroad's sparks and the farmer's crops, again assuming that the farmer had title to the land on which he was growing the crops, the approach offered here would lead to the conclusion that the railroad caused the damage that was experienced by the farmer. But for the fact that the railroad's sparks crossed over onto the farmers land, the crops would not have been destroyed. This can be compared directly to the Coasean view:

> Coase's basic point ... was that if what we meant by causation was but for causation, then both R [the railroad] and F [the farmer] were but for causes of whatever damage is done, for there would be no fire unless the sparks were emitted *and* crops placed near the tracks. (Kelman. p. 584).

It is as if all property lines had been erased, or never existed. The farmer simply chose a plot of land somewhere that had good soil and started planting crops and unfortunately it happened to be near a strip of land that a railroad picked to lay tracks and run train service through. In this sense the Coasean approach to tort is completely void of property rights analysis. Causality is assessed in an institutional vacuum.

As Rizzo and others have pointed out, strict liability is integrally related to causality. In fact its implementation could not proceed without some assessment of causation. By integrating strict liability with catallactic efficiency and the IIS an operational approach to causality can be derived. It is an approach that comes about from a recognition that the issues of property rights and causation cannot be separated.

**The Lack of Property Rights and "Coming to the Nuisance"**

A troublesome area for dealing with problems in tort from the perspective of catallactic efficiency centers on cases where property rights are not clearly defined. As argued in the previous chapter, in general, determining initial entitlements to property is beyond the scope of economic analysis. Fundamentally, since such decisions cannot be ends-independent, ethical arguments must come into play, and in many if not most cases, such decisions must be based entirely on ethical considerations. For the reasons already discussed, cost-benefit analysis of a Coasean nature cannot be a guide. Furthermore, speculation about how initial entitlements might be determined in a Hobbsean state of nature, from behind a "veil of ignorance," is similarly non-operational as a real-world policy guide.

On the other hand, catallactic efficiency can offer some guidance for certain kinds of nuisance problems in tort law. For example, consider the upstream industrial polluter of an unowned river that is being used for recreational purposes downstream. The problem facing a judge in trying to implement the catallactic approach to determining whether the polluter should be held liable in such circumstances, centers on the fact that neither party has title to the river.

In such cases there would be efficiency reasons for invoking a rule of "coming to the nuisance," which suggests that the party that first used the resource should be granted the right to continue to use it. With the problem at hand, the prima facie case would be in favor of whoever was making use of the stream first. The task of the judge and jury would be to sift through the evidence in order to determine whether or not the recreationalists "came to the nuisance."

From the perspective of catallactic efficiency, such a rule, consistently applied, would aid both the market process and the process of individual goal seeking. Its primary efficiency property relates to the certainty that it would provide in the planning and exchange process. If a person is knowingly the first user of an unowned resource, he can feel free to use the resource in a way that will further his goals. A consistently applied rule of coming to the nuisance would add to the first users confidence that his use, if problems arise, will be sanctioned by the courts and that ultimately his plans will be fulfilled and his goals will be accomplished. Of course, this certainty will feed into the knowledge-disseminating aspects of the price system as discussed at various points throughout this book.

Such a rule would also send important signals to potential "comers" to a nuisance. Those signals would aid in the plan formulation process from their perspective, with similar efficiency-enhancing properties for the price system. Clearly, people who expect to use a stream for recreation will not purchase property along that stream if it is being polluted. Similarly, a potentially polluting industry would also be unlikely to purchase land upstream from sites being used for recreation. In both cases, the consequences of their actions would be known, with reasonable confidence, in advance, reducing uncertainty and therefore the potential for errors in the formulation of plans.

Furthermore, a rule of coming to the nuisance would increase the likelihood that a mutually satisfactory bargain might be struck between the potential litigants ex ante, enhancing everyone's goal-seeking activities through expanded exchange. Confident that the rights of the existing user will ultimately be upheld in court, the party that arrives second will face a strong incentive to purchase any rights that he considers worthwhile prior to any litigation.

All this is quite different from the Coasean analysis of coming to the nuisance. The most prominent discussion of this issue from a standard law and economics perspective is by Donald Wittman (1980). Wittman describes the problem as follows:

> It is first necessary to establish the proper sequence of inputs into the productive process (including the production of negative externalities); one must consider who should have been first instead of who was first . . . . Once the efficient sequence is determined, the next step is to determine the liability rule or property right that promotes the efficient sequence. (p. 559)

The analytical approach to these questions is purely in terms of cost-benefit analysis. The answer to the question of who should have been there first varies with how the costs and benefits associated with the competing activities break down. From our perspective this entire approach is a non-starter, for reasons that should be obvious by this point. No outside observer of the market process could ever take the place of the market in determining "the proper sequence of inputs into [a] productive process." This is particularly true in Whittman's analysis where "proper" refers to that sequence which maximizes social efficiency.

Wittman considers coming to the nuisance in a much wider sense than the assessment here. He is not merely examining situations where existing property titles are unclearly defined. On the contrary, in his primary example property titles are not at issue--people building a residential community on property adjacent to a pig farm. As is typical in Coasean analysis, existing property titles are unimportant. Thus the problem we are attempting to solve with a rule of coming to the nuisance, i.e., situations where ownership is not clearly established, is never even an issue. Who actually owns the property over which the conflict exists is an unimportant question.

From the perspective of catallactic efficiency, Wittman's approach could create uncertainties in the formulation of plans and ultimately lead to inefficiencies in the market process. No one could be sure that existing property rights would be upheld in the future. It could not be known with any degree of certainty who one's future neighbors will be or how a future court will resolve the question of "who should have been first."

## CONCLUSION: PROBLEMS AND CONSIDERATIONS FOR FURTHER ANALYSIS

The purpose of this chapter is not to write the final word on issues of tort law or to iron out all the problems that could arise when examining issues in tort from the alternative perspective of catallactic efficiency. The primary purpose has been to illustrate how the alternative theory of externalities developed in the previous chapters can lead to policy analysis that is significantly different from standard analysis. With respect to the economic analysis of tort, the purpose here is to open a door--to introduce a new way of thinking about efficiency when examining approaches to liability and property rights.

There are plenty of unresolved questions and areas yet to be explored. It is hoped that enough interest will ultimately be generated in this mode of analysis to flesh out answers to many of the critical questions that a catallactics approach to law and economics generates.

Generally speaking, some of the most important and interesting questions center on two important areas: the issues of judicial remedies and unclearly defined entitlements. While economics may be able to shed some light on specific aspects of these issues, I believe that a complete solution to problems in these areas will require a non-efficiency based theory of justice.

The question of judicial remedies moves the discussion from the general issue of what kind of liability rule should guide judicial decision making to the specific issue of how that rule should be implemented. From the perspective of catallactic efficiency and its derivative theory of externalities, we can conclude that strict liability, as opposed to negligence, is the rule that should guide the decisions of common law judges and juries. It is the rule that is most consistent with the IIS. But having made a decision of guilt or innocence, how should the problem be resolved?

A number of issues arise in that regard. The first relates to the question of compensation. Can economics be used to determine the amount of damages that should be awarded in any given case? While both the Pigouvian and Coasean paradigms provide solutions to this problem, it has been argued here that these solutions are completely unidentifiable in the real world. Because the standard solutions typically invoke general equilibrium based efficiency criteria, those solutions are unhelpful as a guide to judicial problem solving.

I believe that the theory of catallactic efficiency would not be much more useful in this regard, although the entire issue requires a great deal more consideration and research. Ultimately, this is an issue of corrective justice and clearly must rest on ethical questions of just compensation. My own sentiment holds with that of O'Driscoll and Rizzo, namely that, to the extent possible, the victim should be "made whole." This is consistent with Epstein who explicitly bases his case for strict liability on notions of corrective justice. He argues as a matter of fairness not efficiency, that:

> There is no reason why . . . a defendant in a law suit should be able to shift the loss in question because the [property] belong[s] to someone else. The action in tort in effect enables the injured party to require the defendant to treat the loss he has inflicted on another as though it were his own. (1973, p. 12)

But what making the victim "whole" or requiring the defendant to treat the loss "as though it were his own" means in concrete terms would have to involve ethical judgments that stand apart from questions of efficiency, either economic or catallactic. Because the compensation will probably be monetary does not make it an economic problem.

A second issue that must be dealt with under the rubric of judicial remedies is the relative appropriateness of injunction and damage remedies. This is a specific application of the general problem identified by Calabresi and Melamed, namely choosing between property and liability rules for property rights enforcement. Definitionally:

> An entitlement is protected by a property rule to the extent that someone who wishes to remove the entitlement from its holder must buy it from him in a voluntary transaction in which the value of the entitlement is agreed upon by the seller . . . . Whenever someone may destroy the initial entitlement if he is willing to pay an objectively determined value for it, an entitlement is protected by a liability rule. (Calabresi and Melamed, p. 1092)

Injunction relief, where the generator of the externality is forced to discontinue using the property of the plaintiff, is a direct application of the property rule. A remedy of damage relief only, where the defendant may continue to generate the externality but must compensate the defendant for future damages, is an application of a liability rule.[11] Both are consistent with strict liability.

From a Coasean perspective it is typically argued that when there are only a few parties involved, i.e., when transaction costs are low, injunctions are appropriate. The parties will freely bargain and the efficient solution will be reached. When transaction costs are high, damage relief is appropriate because bargaining will not take place (Cooter and Ulen, 106-108). Again it is assumed that a judge could somehow mimic a Coase theorem solution.

Calabresi and Melamed candidly admit the futility of that approach, using eminent domain as an example to highlight the problems of implementing a liability rule guided by economic efficiency. Recognizing that value is ultimately subjective, they point out that:

> In practice . . . eminent domain simply gives [the plaintiff] what the land is worth "objectively," in the full knowledge that this may result in over or under compensation. (p. 1108).

At first glance, it appears that injunction relief and property rules in general are most consistent with the IIS and therefore catallactic efficiency. But I do not see this conclusion as definitive or necessarily holding in all cases. From the perspective of catallactic efficiency, several issues need to be examined in detail. Primarily, it must be asked how the alternative remedies might affect successful plan formulation. This involves questioning how the alternative approaches would affect uncertainty and whether they would enhance or decrease the possibility of making erroneous decisions in the goal seeking process. Furthermore the impact of the alternative approaches needs to be assessed in terms of their effect on the exchange process and the information flows captured in price movements. The results of these inquiries may be different in different cases or in different categories of cases. Therefore it may not be possible to reach a blanket conclusion concerning one approach vis a vis the other. Clearly, this is fruitful territory for further research.

Furthermore, questions of corrective justice again will likely come into play. This could include considerations of what may be "reasonable" in different situations. But the concept of "reasonableness" must be based, not on the impossible cost-benefit standards of Coasean analysis, but on notions of morality and fairness, even if those concepts cannot be applied with the rigor that only apparently exists in the typical law and economics approach to such issues.

The second broad category of issue that needs much greater attention than was given here is the issue of ambiguous or undefined property titles. While a rule of coming to the nuisance can offer us some help in this area, it most certainly will not apply in all cases. The historical record with regard to the first user may not be clear. Furthermore, there are problems associated with determining entitlements at all to some resources, for example, air, fish in the ocean, etc. Obviously, many of these problems are technological and could be overcome in time. But serious property rights analysis of these issues is just now beginning (see Anderson and Leal).

Again, this is an area where it is unlikely that economics as a science will be able to provide a definitive answer, and economists should be perfectly willing to pass the baton to analysts in other disciplines when disciplinary boundaries are reached. This should be viewed not as an abdication but simply as an honest recognition that all disciplines have domains and certain questions are simply not appropriately or even potentially addressable by economic science.

This point does not negate the primary conclusion of this chapter. As a general approach to problems of tort, strict liability, as a means of strictly enforcing property rights, is more likely to promote catallactic efficiency than is negligence. In the preponderance of cases, the question of who has title to what is clear, and strict liability can be implemented in a relatively straightforward manner. Certainly, there will always be situations that involve subjective considerations of fairness and reasonableness on the part of judges and juries. But this does not imply fundamental problems with using strict liability as a general guide for judicial decision making.

## NOTES

1 For a response to Farrell that makes important distinctions between Coase and Hayek see Boettke (1989).

2 This assumption is made explicit and reiterated at several points during Coase's analysis (see pp. 2, 6, & 32).

3 It has been a consistent part of the Coasean tradition to make this simplifying assumption when discussing issues related to law and economics (See Posner, chapter 1; Polinsky, Chapter 11 and 12). The assumption gives rise to an inherent contradiction when discussing externality problems. By definition, a Pareto-relevant externality is evidence that market conditions are deviating from their long-run equilibrium solutions. If the market-generated prices are truly general equilibrium prices, there would be no problem to analyze. If the externality problem actually exists, then the apparent market prices <u>could not be</u> general equilibrium prices.

4 For a clearly presented example of this see Shavell (1980).

5 Made explicit by Judge Learned Hand in *United States* v. *Carroll Towing Co.*, 159 F. 2d 169 (2d Cir. 1947).

6 It should be pointed out that modifications made to the formula for purposes of analyzing contributory negligence, for example, while important in the Coasean context, do not effect the analysis here.

7 It should be pointed out that Coase himself is inconsistent on this issue. In an earlier article [1981 (1938)] he states that "costs are not necessarily the same as payments. It is this fact that makes the 'costs' disclosed by cost accountants something quite different from 'opportunity costs' . . . . The cost of using [a] machine is the highest receipts that could be obtained by some alternative employment of the machine. This may be any figure and may be unrelated to the cost of the machine" (pp. 108-109). While Coase, in this context, is still conceiving of cost as, at least conceptually measurable, he is clearly implying that the market price of the machine is not likely to be the competitive price.

8 An important issue that typically goes undiscussed relates to the point in time for which cost-benefit calculations should be made. What is the relevant cost configuration? The one that existed at the time of the tort or at the time of the trial? If the court proceedings extend over a lengthy period of time, are the relevant costs calculations those that exist at the beginning or the end of those proceedings? The assumption of general equilibrium prices is tantamount to assuming this problem away.

[9] For a discussion of some of the issues and controversies surrounding this kind of analysis, from within the Coasean framework see Reese, 1989.

[10] For analysis that is explicitly based on this distinction see Whitman, 1980.

[11] Another application of a liability rule is eminent domain.

# CONCLUSION

The framework of analysis offered here represents a radical departure from both standard welfare economics and its application in the area of externalities. For reasons discussed at the outset, and reiterated throughout the text, the perfectly competitive general equilibrium (PCGE) has been completely jettisoned as a normative guide for economic analysis. Furthermore, the focus was not switched to some other end-state result. Instead we began from a recognition of the fact that real-world market processes are open-ended, and that real-world human actors necessarily pursue goals within an open-ended framework of trial and error. In other words, knowledge of means are neither perfect nor "given" to anyone in the system--not market participants, not policy makers, and certainly not economists.

This is a world that differs very significantly from the one that is typically assessed by economists. Following the distinction emphasized by Mises, Hayek, and later, Buchanan, it is a world that is best described as a "catallaxy" not an "economy." It is a setting where individuals, through the process of exchange, pursue goals that are ranked on individually determined value scales. Because these rankings cannot exogenously be fused together or even observed, there is no perspective from which to make value objective. This means that concepts such as social costs and social benefits, and distinctions such as those that are made between private and social costs or benefits, are not only arbitrary, but simply fabrications of the economist's mind.

What is there left to orthodox welfare economics when there is no end state to mimic and when the full implications of subjective value are taken seriously? Certainly, in the area of externalities analysis, very little remains. The orthodox approach to efficiency is wholly dependent on these concepts. As a consequence, most of the market failure-based approaches to public policy, which are derived from considerations of "economic" efficiency as traditionally defined, are totally dependent on social cost-benefit analysis and a general equilibrium benchmark.

The Pigouvian approach to both defining and resolving externality problems is completely undermined when the foundation provided by a perfectly competitive general equilibrium is withdrawn. Outside of this framework the orthodox tax and subsidy approach to such issues is vacuous. It becomes clear that economic efficiency-based arguments for pollution taxes, energy taxes, effluent charges, etc., crumble without the PCGE touchstone. The same is true for the standard market failure arguments that are made for the subsidization or government provision of so-called public goods, such as education, roads, parks, or even police and national defense. Without the benchmark of a PCGE these excise taxes and subsidies are stripped of their alleged efficiency properties.

As was noted in the last chapter, the same assessment applies to Coasean type property rights analysis and its policy prescriptions in the field of law and economics. While Coase presented his analysis of harmful effects as both a criticism of and alternative to Pigouvian analysis, its policy prescriptions are no less dependent on the results associated with a PCGE. It is only an alternative to standard analysis within the general equilibrium framework. Our attempt here has been to break free of this paradigm.

The primary question that has been addressed here is, what should welfare economics and, in particular, externalities analysis look like when the full implications of an open-ended market process are considered. This should not be viewed as an attempt to formulate the last word on either welfare economics or externalities theory from this perspective. Quite the contrary. The purpose has been to lay the groundwork for research in the entire range of areas that have typically fallen under the rubric of externalities. In this sense, the purpose here has been to open doors, not to close them, although I emphatically believe that the door should be closed on the entire concept of perfect competition as a meaningful guide for normative questions in economics.

Economists who have emphasized market process analysis in considering questions of welfare economics have for many years focussed on issues related to industrial organization and especially monopoly and competition. Since Hayek's work on knowledge and the importance of information in the 1930s and '40s, a consistent theme of the Austrian school has been that the twin pillars of general equilibrium and perfect competition are useless as a real world policy guide. The theoretical work of Hayek and Kirzner, and the empirical analysis in the area of anti-trust of Armentano has had an important, although somewhat limited, influence on the economics profession at large. That work has done a great deal to shift the emphasis away from pure market structure analysis that stresses comparative statics when dealing with issues in industrial organization, and toward a concern for real-world market processes.[1]

While many economists have recognized that the Austrian criticisms of standard welfare economics have implications for developing an alternative approach to competition and monopoly, this has not been the case when it comes to externalities. For the most part, Austrian-type analysis of the issue have ended at the criticism stage and have had very little impact on the profession at large. I think that this is mostly because, unlike the area of competition and monopoly, no positive alternative has been offered. The typical procedure, with few exceptions (see Rizzo, 1980A), has been to critically assess the analysis in one area or another related to externalities, and then conclude that the entire issue is outside of the framework of economic analysis and is more appropriately the subject of ethics.[2]

While I see the scope for economic analysis in this area to be much more narrow than is acknowledged in the standard literature, the idea that externalities is a subject area that is completely beyond the range of efficiency analysis is incorrect, although, as in the area of competition, the meaning of efficiency has had to be reconstructed to fit the realities of an open-ended world.

## UNRESOLVED ISSUES

Opportunities for further research in this area are without limit. As already emphasized, the purpose here has been to open a door--to provide an alternative framework of analysis for interpreting not only externality problems, but other areas in welfare economics, including competition and monopoly.

There are vast numbers of issues, both theoretical and empirical that one can begin to address. On a theoretical level it is clear that the relationship between normative economics and ethics in general needs to be explored more thoroughly. As we have pursued our analysis here the limits of economic science were continuously being felt as a binding constraint, particularly when it came to the issue of establishing initial entitlements. This suggests that ethics will have to play a significant role if we expect to offer a complete normative analysis of the externalities question, particularly if we are to proceed within the methodological constraints imposed by Austrian economics. As argued here, those are nothing more than the same constraints imposed by reality. To ignore them, as is done in Pigouvian welfare economics, does not make them any less binding. It simply makes the analysis less meaningful and, therefore, less relevant.

It was argued that in dealing with certain issues in tort that economics could inform judges and juries in some instances where property rights are not clearly delineated. Hence we argued that a rule of "coming to the nuisance" would promote catallactic efficiency in certain cases where title to resources under conflict were not clear. But this may not be relevant in all or even most situations where property titles are ambiguously defined. It may not be clear who actually made use of the property first and, furthermore, non-economic considerations may override the first-use principle. My own feeling is that, as particular kinds of externality problems are explored in light of catallactic efficiency, different ways in which efficiency analysis can inform the ethical decisions concerning initial entitlements will be discovered. No doubt though, there will always be unexplored questions concerning the relationship between economic analysis and ethical analysis.

By invoking Hayek's rule that normative economic analysis must remain "ends independent," we have at least helped to sharpen what has become a very blurred boundary between the disciplines of ethics and economics. Once Hayek's constraint is imposed on normative economic analysis it becomes clear that the border between economics and ethics is crossed regularly by economists--typically without them even recognizing the transgression. Every time an economist views policy analysis in terms of social costs and benefits, the ends of different actors are being compared to determine their relative "value" to society. From the perspective taken in this book, this is inherently an ethical question, the answer to which cannot be grounded in economics.

On both a theoretical and practical level, it would be important to explore the issue of "second best" within a framework of catallactic efficiency. Certainly there are and will be many cases where the IIS, for technological or political reasons, cannot be conformed to. In these situations it would be important to develop alternative approaches to the problem that would minimize the damage done to the market process.

In this regard several problems come to mind. The first is with respect to situations where the generator of the externality may not be easily identified. An example of this, to the extent that it is truly a problem, would be acid rain.[3] In most cases perceived problems caused by acid rain cannot be traced to specific polluters. Technology is such that, at best, acid rain can be attributed to general categories of polluters in specific regions. In cases where such "identification" problems exist and solutions that are consistent with the IIS in all respects might be impossible to implement, it would be important to develop a second best approach. While it might be necessary to consider a general theory of second best that highlights the policy goals in terms of catallactic efficiency, second best solutions would probably have to be developed case by case.

A second, but related, problem occurs when there are large numbers of people generating an externality, each contributing an imperceptible amount to the problem. An example of this is urban smog caused by auto emissions. Here again, the kind of specific identification that would be necessary in order to implement a solution that is completely consistent with the IIS might be impossible. The problem here though may be more political than technological. Rothbard (1982A) has suggested that this particular problem is exacerbated by the fact that the roads are publicly owned. If the roads were privately owned, the owners, not the drivers, would be held responsible for damage caused by any pollutants emitted from the authorized use of their property. This would encourage the road owners to set emission control standards for automobiles that use their roads. Clearly a major stumbling block to such an approach is that the electorate is unlikely to be willing to accept the wholesale privatization of roads.

Politically acceptable second best solutions that move in the direction suggested here can be developed. A promising approach has been noted by Anderson and Leal. They suggest a "system of tradable pollution permits:"

> Under this system, a pollution control agency would issue a limited number of permits authorizing the discharge of a specific amount of pollutants. The number of permits would determine the level of [pollution] . . . . [T]his system will ensure that a given level of control can be achieved efficiently through a market for the permits. (p. 145)[4]

The point here is that this kind of innovative thinking will be necessary if the Austrian approach to externalities is to become a relevant part of public policy debates.

It should be pointed out that both the Pigouvian and Coasean analysis face similar "identification" problems in implementing their specific solutions. In either case, the necessary cost calculations, even if theoretically sound, could not be made without being able to identify both the specific polluters and those who are bearing the cost of the pollution. While most economists would argue that effluent charges might be appropriate in such cases, the argument for such charges in most instances is not made on strictly Pigouvian grounds.[5] First it is often claimed that effluent charges would be less costly to administer than direct regulation of emissions (Stroup and Baden). Second, it is argued that the polluters would respond to the tax in the same way that they would respond to a factor price. Emissions would be reduced in a way that is most efficient given the production and cost functions of the particular firm. It would allow each firm to "adjust to their most efficient level of pollution control," given the amount of the tax (Stroup and Baden, p. 88). As one proponent of effluent charges has candidly admitted:

> ... economists have moved to the position of advocating effluent charges as a means of meeting politically determined environmental standards at minimum cost. (Orr, p. 57)

That is a far cry from the claim that pollution taxes can be used in a way that will maximize social efficiency. Economists have simply relegated themselves to the role of telling politicians the cheapest way to achieve politically determined goals. As the study of public choice suggests, this becomes advice not on how to maximize "social welfare" but advice on how to maximize the welfare of the politicians, bureaucrats, and special interests that win out in the political decisions-making process.

An issue that has been left, in large part, open in this book concerns the origins of institutions, such as police and courts, that are necessary for the establishment and maintenance of the IIS. In other words, the analysis presented here does not automatically lead to a justification of the state--even a minimal state. As discussed in Chapter 4, orthodox market failure and public goods theory, while purporting to provide such a justification, actually does not. Standard public goods theory and the analysis of free rider problems implicitly must assume that property rights and the right to make contracts exist, but for certain other reasons--free riders, non-excludability, etc.--some exchanges that "should" take place do not. In other words, while claiming to provide a justification for the state, some institutions with the capability of establishing property rights must already exist for analysis to proceed. In order to talk about transaction-cost problems, which are at the root of all public goods issues, if not all externalities problems (see Coase, 1960), one must assume that people have the right to transact.

Whether a coercive state should or should not exist to set up, maintain, and enforce the IIS is not a question that a theory of externalities or even efficiency can answer. One can only talk about catallactic efficiency within the context of a catallaxy. Therefore, some sense of private property and some form of rights and contract enforcement are necessary pre-conditions of the analysis.

Surely, economists have not proven in any empirical sense that institutions such as police and courts, either criminal or civil, would not arise without coercive state intervention. Recent work by Bruce L. Benson (1990) suggests that the standard arguments are, in fact, not borne out historically. Benson researches and reveals case after case where everything from the establishment of property rights to their enforcement and adjudication have arisen completely from voluntary cooperation, without the presence of state intervention or even the existence of a state.

Benson's research has profound implications from the perspective of the theory presented in this book. Catallactic efficiency does not necessarily provide a starting point from which one can argue for or against the existence of a state. On the other hand, this notion of efficiency only becomes relevant within the context of a market-oriented society. If a society decides, through whatever process, to invoke catallactic efficiency and the achievement of individually determined goals as a welfare norm, it must also be concerned about establishing the institutions that are necessary for a catallaxy to exist. In fact, this is the issue currently facing citizens in the predominantly non-market societies of Eastern Europe. Certainly the analysis here suggests that the most consistent means of establishing such institutions would be through totally voluntary efforts. What Benson has shown is that the traditional economic theory, which suggests that such voluntary solutions could not come about, does not hold up when measured against the historical evidence.

## FINAL REMARKS

Modern welfare economics has been developed in such a way as to ultimately have very little relevance for real-world policy making. In constructing their model of efficiency economists have abstracted almost completely from the real-world efficiency problem faced by individual human actors. In the market process there are real human beings, not the robot-like "agents" in most economic models, who must cope with the world as it actually exists. To be relevant, welfare economics must take into account the fact that human activity takes place through time. Therefore the pursuit of ends and the formulation and execution of plans is strictly an open-ended process of trial and error. New information is always being revealed. This new information may help to reaffirm our existing set of plans or it may be cause for either minor or radical revision. This is the efficiency problem facing us all, and any theory of social efficiency must spring from a recognition of this fact.

Unfortunately, modern theories of economic welfare, which are based on notions of perfect competition and general equilibrium, completely abstract from the fundamental efficiency problem. What economists have done is constructed a parallel universe that looks very little like the one with which we must cope, and assessed the efficiency problem that would exist in that universe. It is an efficiency problem that can be formalized and mathematized relatively easily. Within the context of this "other world," neat and unambiguous solutions can be derived for any problem that might arise. Unfortunately, the economist insists that this entire analysis is something more than a mental exercise, and pretends that his parallel universe is actually the world in which we live. Taxes, subsidies, antitrust laws, public utility regulations, etc., all of which very neatly solve problems that arise in the economist's model, are presented to policy makers without any recognition of the fact that they were developed within a context that bears very little resemblance to the real world.

It is time that economists put an end to this charade. The world of perfect competition has no relevance for real-world policy making, and it should be purged as a foundation for welfare economics. Such a purge would have profound implications for the way economists practice their trade--particularly in public policy-related fields like public finance, law and economics, and industrial organization. The role of mathematics and econometrics would be seriously reduced. The focus of analysis would be taken away from particular market outcomes and placed on the processes and individual activities that have led to those outcomes. As part of this, most public policy analysis would assess the kinds of rules that economic activities must operate under. Even if one does not adopt the particular form of welfare economics that has been presented here, in general this is the nature of the analysis that is appropriate when the "open-endedness" of market activities is fully considered.

## NOTES

1 As an example of this influence, it is becoming increasingly common for introductory economics texts to discuss the notion of competition as a process as an alternative to the standard approach (Ekelund and Tollison, 1991; Gwartney and Stroup, 1990). For other examples of influence on non-Austrian writers in this area see Brozen (1982), Ekelund and Sauerman (1988), and Shughart (1990).

2 See papers by Rothbard and Egger in Rizzo, ed. (1979). For a follow-up application of an ethical approach often endorsed by Austrians see Rothbard (1982A). Also see Kirzner, 1989.

3 Recent research has suggested that acid rain may not be a policy-relevant externality in the sense discussed here; see Krug (1990).

4 Much of Anderson and Leal's work, while not specifically relying upon the kind of externalities analysis presented here, can be viewed as an application of the IIS to specific environmental problems. Many problems similar to those being discussed here are considered and property rights based solutions are suggested. Anderson and Leal's work is specifically notable because it takes into account many of the knowledge problems and subjective value problems emphasized here.

5 For an exception see Wallace Oates (1988) who argues as if there are no insurmountable problems, either conceptually or practically, with implementing effluent charges that will, presumably unambiguously, enhance economic efficiency. Others, while noting many of the problems discussed here, choose to ignore them or not take them seriously. [See Kneese (1977), and Baumol (1970)].

## REFERENCES


Ackerman, Bruce A. and Hassler, William T. 1981. *Clean Coal/Dirty Air*. New Haven and London: Yale University Press.

Anderson, Terry L. and Leal, Donald R. 1991. *Free Market Environmentalism*. San Francisco: Pacific Research Institute for Public Policy.

Armentano, Dominick T. 1990. *Antitrust and Monopoly: Anatomy of a Policy Failure*, 2nd ed.. New York and London: Holmes and Meier.

Baumol, William. 1970. Review of Buchanan (1969) *Cost and Choice*, in *The Journal of Economic Literature*. Vol. VIII No. 4.

__________ and Oates, Wallace E. 1975. *The Theory of Environmental Policy*. Englewood Cliffs, N.J.: Prentice Hall.

Benson, Bruce L. 1990. *The Enterprise of Law*. San Francisco: Pacific Research Institute for Public Policy.

Block, Walter. 1983. "Public Goods and Externalities: The Case of Roads." *The Journal of Libertarian Studies*. Vol. VII No. 1.

Bohm-Bawerk, Eugen von. 1962. *Shorter Classics of Bohm-Bawerk*, Vol. I. South Holland, Ill.: Libertarian Press.

Boettke, Peter. 1989. "Comment on Joseph Farrell, Information and the Coase Theorem." *Journal of Economic Perspectives*. Vol. 3, No. 2.

__________. 1990. *The Political Economy of Soviet Socialism: The Formative Year, 1918-1928*. Boston and London: Kluwer Academic Publishers.

Brownstein, Barry P. 1980. "Pareto Optimality, External Benefits, and Public Goods: A Subjectivist Approach." *The Journal of Libertarian Studies*. Vol. IV, No.1.

Brozen, Yale. 1982. *Concentration, Mergers, and Public Policy*. New York: Macmillan Publishers.

Buchanan, James. 1969. *Cost and Choice*. Chicago: Markham Press.

__________. 1975. *The Limits of Liberty*. Chicago: University of Chicago Press.

__________. 1979A. "Natural and Artifactual Man" in *What Should Economists Do?* Indianapolis: Liberty Press.

_________. 1979B. "What Should Economists Do?" in *What Should Economists Do?...*

_________. 1981. "Introduction: L.S.E. Cost Theory in Retrospect." Buchanan and Thirlby, ed., *L.S.E. Essays on Cost.* New York and London: New York University Press.

_________ and Stubblebine, William Craig. 1962. "Externality." *Economica.* Vol. 29 No. 116.

Butos, William. 1985. "Menger: A Suggested Interpretation." *The Atlantic Economic Journal.* Vol. 13 No. 2.

Calabresi, Guido and Melamed, Douglas. 1972. "Property Rules, Liability Rules, and Inalienability: One View of the Cathedral." *Harvard Law Review.* Vol. 85, No. 6.

Coase, Ronald H.. 1960. "The Problem of Social Costs." *Journal of Law and Economics.* Vol. 3. (October).

_________. 1981 (1938). "Business Organization and the Accountant" in Buchanan and Thirlby, ed., ...

Cooter, Robert and Ulen, Thomas. 1988. *Law and Economics.* Glenview, Il. and London: Scott, Foresman and Co.

Cordato, Roy E. 1980. "The Austrian Theory of Efficiency and the Role of Government." *The Journal of Libertarian Studies.* Vol. 4, No. 4.

_________. 1987. *An Analysis of Externalities in Austrian Economics.* Unpublished doctoral dissertation. George Mason University.

_________. 1989. "Subjective Value, Time Passage, and the Economics of Harmful Effects." *The Hamline Law Review.* Vol.12, No. 2.

_________. 1992. "Energy Taxes, Externalities, and the Pretence of Efficiency." Paper prepared for the Cato Institute, Washington, D.C., conference on energy policy, January 16, 1992.

Demsetz, Harold. 1979. "Ethics and Efficiency in Property Rights Systems." in Rizzo, ed. *Time, Uncertainty, and Disequilibrium.* Lexington, Mass.: Lexington Books.

Dolan, Edwin, ed. 1976. *The Foundations of Modern Austrian Economics.* Kansas City: Sheed and Ward.

Egger, John B. 1979. "Efficiency is Not a Substitute for Ethics" in Rizzo, ed. *Time, Uncertainty...*

Ekelund, Robert and Saurman, David. 1988. *Advertising and the Market Process.* San Francisco: The Pacific Institute.

_________ and Tollison, Robert. 1991. *Economics*, 3rd ed. New York: Harper Collins, Publishers.

Epstein, Richard. 1973. "A Theory of Strict Liability." *The Journal of Legal Studies.* Vol. II No. 1. Page numbers from reprint with the same title. Washington: Cato Institute. 1980.

_________. 1974. "Defenses and Subsequent Pleas in a Theory of Strict Liability." *The Journal of Legal Studies.* Vol. III. No. 1.

_________. 1975. "Intentional Harms." *The Journal of Legal Studies.* Vol. IV No. 3.

_________. 1979. "Nuisance Law: Corrective Justice and Its Utilitarian Constraints." *The Journal of Legal Studies.* Vol. VIII, No. 1.

Farrell, Joseph. 1987. "Information and the Coase Theorm." *The Journal of Economic Perspectives.* Vol. 1, No. 1.

Friedman, David. 1973. *The Machinery of Freedom.* New York: Harper and Row.

Garrison, Roger. 1978. "Austrian Macroeconomics" in Spadaro, ed. *New Directions in Austrian Economics.* Kansas City: Sheed, Andrews, and McMeel.

Gwartney, James D. and Stroup, Richard L. 1990. *Economics: Private and Public Choice.* New York: Harcourt Brace Jovanovich, Publishers.

Goodman, John C. 1978. "An Economic Theory of the Evolution of the Common Law." *The Journal of Legal Studies.* Vol. VII, No. 2.

Hayek, F.A. 1948 (1935A). "Socialist Calculation I: The State of the Debate" in *Individualism and Economic Order.* South Bend Indiana: Gateway Editions, Ltd. Reprinted from *Collectivist Economic Planning.* London: George Rutledge and Sons, Ltd.

_________. 1948 (1935B). "Socialist Calculation II: The State of the Debate" in *Individualism....* Reprinted from *Collectivist...*

_________. 1948 (1945A). "The Use of Knowledge in Society," in *Individualism....* Reprinted from *The American Economic Review.* Vol. XXXV, No. 4.

_________. 1948 (1945B). "Socialist Calculation III: The Competitive Solution" in *Individualism....* Reprinted from *Economica.* Vol. VII. No. 26.

_________. 1948. "The Meaning of Competition" in *Individualism...*

_________. 1955. *The Counter-Revolution of Science.* Glencoe, Ill.: The Free Press.

_________. 1960. *The Constitution of Liberty.* Chicago: University of Chicago Press.

_________. 1967 (1935). *Prices and Production.* New York Augustus M. Kelly.

_________. 1976. *Law, Legislation and Liberty*, Vol. 2. Chicago: University of Chicago Press.

_________. 1979. _________, Vol. 3. Chicago: University of Chicago Press.

_________. 1985. *New Studies in Philosophy, Politics, Economics and the History of Ideas.* Chicago: University of Chicago Press.

High, Jack. 1985. "State Education: Have Economists Made a Case." *The Cato Journal.* Vol. 5 No. 1.

_________. 1986. "Equilibrium and Disequilibrium in the Market Process" in Israel Kirzner, ed. *Subjectivism, Intelligibility, and Economic Understanding.* New York: New York University Press.

Huber, Peter W. 1988. *Liability: The Legal Revolution and Its Consequences.* New York: Basic Books, Inc.

Kelman, Mark. 1987. "The Necessary Myth of Objective Causation Judgments in Liberal Political Theory." *Chicago-Kent Law Review*, Vol. 63.

Kirzner, Israel. 1963. *Market Theory and the Price System.* Princeton, N.J.: D. Van Nostrand Co., Inc.

_________. 1973. *Competition and Entrepreneurship.* Chicago: University of Chicago Press.

_________. 1976. "On the Method of Austrian Economics" in Edwin Dolan, ed. *The Foundations...*

_________. 1979. *Perception, Opportunity, and Profit.* Chicago: University of Chicago Press.

_________, ed. 1982. *Method, Process, and Austrian Economics.* Lexington, Mass.: Lexington Books.

_________. 1985. "The Perils of Regulation: A Market Process Approach" in *Discovery and the Capitalist Process.* Chicago: University of Chicago Press.

_________. 1988A. "Welfare Economics: A Modern Austrian Perspective" in Block and Rockwell, ed., *Man, Economy, and Liberty: Essays in Honor of Murray N. Rothbard.* Auburn, Al.: The Ludwig von Mises Institute.

_________. 1988B. "Foreword: Advertising in an Open Ended Universe," foreword to Ekelund and Saurman, *Advertising....*

_________. 1989. *Discovery, Capitalism, and Distributive Justice.* New York: Basil Blackwell.

Kneese, Allen V. 1977. *Economics and the Environment.* New York: Penguin Books.

Krug, Edward C. 1991. "The Great Acid Rain Flimflam." *Policy Review*, No. 52, Spring.

Lachmann, Ludwig. 1969. "Methodological Individualism and the Market Economy" in Erich Streissler, et.al., ed. *Roads to Freedom: Essays in Honor of Friedrich A. Hayek.* London: Routledge and Kegan Paul.

_________. 1976. "On the Central Concept of Austrian Economics" in Dolan, ed. Foundations...

Lavoie, Don. 1985. *National Economic Planning: What is Left?* Cambridge, Mass.: Ballinger Publishing Co.

Lewin, Peter. 1982. "Pollution Externalities, Social Costs and Strict Liability." *Cato Journal.* Vol. 2 No. 1.

Lipsey, R.G. and Lancaster, R.K. 1957. "The General Theory of Second Best." *The Review of Economic Studies*, Vol. 24, No. 63.

Littlechild, S.C. 1978. "The Problem of Social Cost" in Spadaro, ed. *New Directions...*

_________. 1979. *The Fallacy of the Mixed Economy.* Washington, D.C.: The Cato Institute.

Marshall, Alfred. 1947 (1890). *Principles of Economics.* London: Macmillan.

Menger, Carl. 1981 (1870). *Principles of Economics.* New York: New York University Press.

Mises, Ludwig von. 1966 (1949). *Human Action.* Chicago: Contemporary Books, Inc.

_________. 1978. *Liberalism.* Kansas City: Sheed, Andrews and McMeel.

_________. 1981 (1922). *Socialism.* Indianapolis: Liberty Classics.

Mishan, E.J. 1971. "The Post War Literature on Externalities: An Interpretive Essay." *The Journal of Economic Literature.* Vol. 9 No. 8.

_________. 1973. *Economics for Social Decisions.* New York: Praeger Publishers.

Musgrave, Richard A. and Peacock, Alan T. 1958. *Classics in the Theory of Public Finance.* London and New York: Macmillan.

Myrdal, Gunnar. 1955. *The Political Element in the Development of Economic Theory.* Cambridge, Mass.: Harvard University Press.

Neck, Reinhard. 1985. "Emil Sax's Contributions to Public Economics." unpublished manuscript.

Nozick, Robert. 1974. *Anarchy, State, and Utopia.* New York: Basic Books, Inc.

Oates, Wallace E. 1988. "A Pollution Tax Makes Sense," in Herbert Stein, ed. *Tax Policy in the Twenty-First Century.* New York: John Wiley and Sons.

O'Driscoll, Gerald P. 1977. *Economics as a Coordination Problem.* Kansas City: Sheed, Andrews and McMeel.

_________ and Rizzo, Mario J. 1985. *The Economics of Time and Ignorance.* Oxford: Basil Blackwell.

Orr, Lloyd D. 1981. "Social Costs, Incentive Structures, and Environmental Policies" in John Baden and Richard Stroup, ed. *Bureaucracy vs. Environment.* Ann Arbor: University of Michigan Press.

Osterfeld, David. 1987. "'Social Utility' and Government Transfers of Wealth: An Austrian Perspective." *The Review of Austrian Economics*, Vol. 2.

Palmer, Tom G. 1989. "Intellectual Property: A Non-Posnerian Law and Economics Approach." *Hamline Law Review.* Vol. 12, No. 2.

Pigou, A.C. 1952. *The Economics of Welfare.* 4th ed. London: Macmillan.

Polinsky, A. Mitchell. 1983. *An Introduction to Law and Economics.* Boston: Little Brown and Co.

Posner, Richard. 1973. *Economic Analysis of the Law.* Boston: Little Brown and Co.

Priest, George L. 1977. "The Common Law Process and the Selection of Efficient Rules." *The Journal of Legal Studies*, Vol. IV, No. 1.

Reese, David A. 1989. "Does the Common Law Evolve?" *Hamline Law Review*, Vol. 12, No. 2.

Rizzo, Mario J. 1979. "Uncertainty, Subjectivity, and the Economic Analysis of Law," in Rizzo, ed. *Time, Uncertainty and Disequilibrium.* Lexington, Mass: Lexington Books.

_________. 1980A. "Law Amid Flux: The Economics of Negligence and Strict Liability." *Journal of Legal Studies.* Vol. 9 No. 2.

_________. 1980B. "Foreword" to Richard Epstein's *A Theory of Strict Liability.* Washington D.C.: Cato Institute.

_________. 1980C. "The Mirage of Efficiency." *Hofstra Law Review*, Vol. 8, No. 3.

Rothbard, Murray. 1962. *Man Economy and State.* Los Angeles: Nash.

_________. 1970. *Power and Market.* Kansas City: Sheed, Andrews and McMeel, Inc.

_________. 1973A. *For A New Liberty.* New York: Macmillan.

_________. 1973B. "Value Implications of Economic Theory." *The American Economist*. Vol. 17, Spring.

_________. 1976. "Praxeology, Value Judgments, and Public Policy," in Dolan, ed., *The Foundations....*

_________. 1977. *A Reconstruction of Utility and Welfare Economics*. New York: Center for Libertarian Studies. Originally published in, Mary Sennholz, ed. *On Freedom and Free Enterprise*. Princeton, N.J.: Van Nostrand, 1956.

_________. 1979. "Comment: The Myth of Efficiency" in Rizzo, ed. *Time, Uncertainty...*

_________. 1982A. "Law, Property Rights and Air Pollution." *The Cato Journal*. Vol. 2 No. 1.

_________. 1982B. *The Ethics of Liberty*. Atlantic Highlands, N.J.: Humanities Press.

Rubin, Paul H. 1977. "Why is the Common Law Efficient?" *The Journal of Legal Studies*, Vol. IV, No. 1.

Samuelson, Paul. 1954. "The Pure Theory of Public Expenditures." *Review of Economics and Statistics*. Vol. 36 No. 4.

Selgin, George A. 1988. *The Theory of Free Banking: Money Supply Under Competitive Note Issue*. Totowa, N.J.: Rowman and Littlefield.

Shavell, Steven. 1980. "Strict Liability vs. Negligence." Journal of Legal Studies, Vol. 4, No. 1.

Shughart, William. 1990. *The Organization of Industry*. Homewood, Il.: Richard D. Irwin.

Stroup, Richard and Baden, John. 1983. *Natural Resources. Bureaucratic Myths and Environmental Management*. San Francisco: Pacific Institute for Public Policy Research.

Vaughn, Karen. 1980. "Does it Matter that Costs are Subjective?" *Southern Economics Journal*. Vol. 46, No. 3.

Viner, Jacob. 1953 (1931). "Cost Curves and Supply Curves" in *Readings in Price Theory*. New York: Blakiston Co.

Weber, Wilhelm. 1973. "Collective Goods and the Planning of Fiscal Programs," in *Carl Menger and the Austrian School of Economics*. ed. J.R. Hicks and W. Weber. Oxford: Clarendon Press.

Wieser, Friedrich von. 1967. *Social Economics*. New York: Augustus M. Kelley.

White, Lawrence H. 1984.· *Free Banking in Britain: Theory Experience and Debate 1800-1845*. Cambridge: Cambridge University Press.

Wittman, Donald. 1980. "First Come, First Served: An Economic Analysis of 'Coming to the Nuisance'." *The Journal of Legal Studies*, Vol. IX, No. 3.

# INDEX

MIX
Papier aus verantwortungsvollen Quellen
Paper from responsible sources
FSC® C105338

If you have any concerns about our products,
you can contact us on
**ProductSafety@springernature.com**

In case Publisher is established outside the EU,
the EU authorized representative is:
**Springer Nature Customer Service Center GmbH**
**Europaplatz 3, 69115 Heidelberg, Germany**

Printed by Libri Plureos GmbH
in Hamburg, Germany